THE BRIGHT
MORNING STAR

THE BRIGHT MORNING STAR

Leslie Jerry Williams
and
Corinne Williams

To order additional copies of this book, contact:
Xlibris Corporation
1-888-795-4274
www.Xlibris.com
Orders@Xlibris.com
113348

CONTENTS

PREFACE

I can't make you read this book. I can't make you like what you read I can only write what I hear and see.

I don't even like to write, except when the spirit touches me. Then I only write what he's telling me. Yet he knows all won't hear and see this writing he has given to you and me. If only some will take the time to read this page he has given to me, then maybe one will be able to really see and understand that the Lord is talking to you through me.

Lots of people will say I don't care; what they mean is that they can't see because will I write what they want to see? I think not.

I only write what is told to me, and what to say is given to me from the one known as the Living Tree, the one that touches your heart and mine!

So please I want to reaffirm if this is for you. You will know and see that what is said here is not from me but something from the Lord—something he wants you to hear and see. You don't even know of me.

I'm the one from a distant land, calling out from where I stand to touch the hearts of the Lord's chosen, woman and man. I write with the ink that he put into my hand that I may spread his word across this great land.

The Lord loves you and wants to take your hand. The Lord speaks. I respond. I have faith you will hear his song and search your heart as you read this Psalm. For he would really like for you to come along!

So I only have this to say, if you got this far, you may as well go all the way. Read the book or at least take a look.

L. J. Williams
© 1999

9

INTRODUCTION

I make no claim as to what I've got, only thoughts I feel should be taught in this life so that some may see the light of day: the love of God and the love he has for you and me.

His son Jesus started this work when he died on the cross for the likes of you and me.

He sent his people out across this great land to tell all people of his Father's great plan to give forgiveness to all who can stand and reach out to others when he takes them by the hand.

We each come to the Lord as we each have our day—some to judgment, some to pray.

He never promised it would be easy. He did promise he would teach them to pray and that he would always be near, if we would only see and hear.

You ask, "How do you see and hear what can't be seen and makes no sound?" Sight is by faith. Look around.

Did you make this day or the flowers or the ground? In fact, did you give yourself the ability to talk or praise the Lord, the Lord your God?

Think of God and not so much of your-self, for this is his day. For remember, you are made of clay.

So keep in mind when you see this book that it's time to praise the Lord that he found you in time, that he gives you, through free choice, the right to walk his way or the right to decline. Let me say here that if you feel the love of God, please read this book. If not, please don't waste your time, for your time will soon pass away.

There is one more thing the Holy Spirit has to say. Have a God-loving day as you go on your way today knowing I spoke to you today. That's what he said to say to you today.

Start with John of the Bible; he spoke of the way two thousand years before today.

"Praise God," that's what he said to say to you today.

ACKNOWLEDGMENT

I can only praise my Lord for the words and thoughts that flow from the point of my pen.

For I somehow never know the thought or theme of what I write as though it's a dream until it's done. Then I read it to see what it means and how it fits into God's plans for his creation of which he calls mortal men, whom he made and named before time began. As I say, I'm glad that I can call the Lord my friend, for he walked with me in his death so that he could walk with me in this life.

This brings up a recall. I might add thanks to my friends and my wife. All the works in this writings of death, dying, living, and life as well! As the reasons to have your God your Lord, as well as the role of the Holy Spirit in the meaning of life! Without them, there is no meaning to the question of life—only the deep dark hole and the stillness of death!

So in closing this note, I would like you to see a small trinity of the spirit, my wife and me if you can really see.

TO SEE OR NOT TO BE

The sphere of heaven as well as earth can only be seen as a half at a time, kind of like day and night or wrong and right. The God of the universe made all that is visible to hide the unseen, for everything missed is something gained; they in the big circle call that the zigzag or yin and yang, the in and out, top and bottom. But really, God made all these things for us to have or have not.

On the midnight clear, two thousand years ago, three wise men followed a star of prominence to somewhere near here to a time of birth of life for the world to know great joy. At the same time knowing that his son must die to save the world from the bad, God only wants the good for us, but in God's realm, in the sphere of here or not here, take a look. Tell me what you see, tell me what you hear. Do you feel what you can't see? Do you hear or just believe? I tell you, believe even if you can't see, believe even if you can't hear. Believe in your heart for the son of God. Believe in things you see? Believe in God above. Also believe in me, the son of the Father, the spirit of God. If you seek, you will plainly see. With God, all things are possible, even to touch the untouchable. To see the invisible and, yes, to hear the voice of God as well. With God, who is there to fear, reach out, touch, the hand of God, your Lord. He is standing right here. He is near. The other sphere

He holds the scepter of far and near, sees a lifetime in the twinkle of the eye, and holds the stars in his mighty right hand, lets them fall like grains of sand, then turns them to drops of rain, to begin all over again.

Ask of him, Jesus, our Lord. He'll give you a new life again. Yes, a treasure he will give to thee and graft you in to his living tree.

Eternity, can you see? That's what my Lord said to say. Also, have a nice day.

A Friend

BIRTH OF THE STAR

It's soon to be the birthday of our savior, Christ, our Lord. He brought joy to the world for all that could see and peace on earth for those that hear the message, gave out on the midnight clear, goodwill toward men.

A promise from God, as he gave us his son, a babe in a manger he gave us that year. Knowing his son would die for us, according to his plan that upon the cross, God might again welcome his creation, man.

To forgive us, that his son might take our hand as he guides us through life on the way to the promise, a tour if you will, of the valleys and the hills. The chills as well as the thrills, as we learn fellowship and what it can mean as we hold the hand of God as we marvel at the miracles of the seen and unseen. For remember, we also have the "spirit" the Holy One of God. The spirit of his son, that's still alive, sitting on his throne. He guides us on our way to this very day, from his death nearly two thousand years ago.

The devil thought he had won on that day. That Christ Jesus died on that cross, not knowing the power of God's great plan and the raising up again of the spirit of his son, only then realizing that God had won, in giving of his love to his son. That the resurrection of the son would place him on the throne and the "love of God" would to this day still carry on.

Watch the morning star, the star, of David as it appears, for it was said of Jesus our Lord, "I, Jesus, have sent my angel to give you this message. I Am both the source of David and the heir to his throne. I Am the bright morning star."

Praise God again,
A Friend

I was Lost

It's hard sometimes, to say where I've been. In fact at times I've been there and back again and was not aware I was lost in sin. Was not aware how I'd got back again.

Sometimes it's hard on the mind. When you, get hit with a rod.

Not once in a while, I mean every time, I'm slow. Well, not that slow. I do learn after a few times which way I go. I hear a voice inside that tells me, I Am the way. I hear myself say, "Who said that?" But that was the day before yesterday, and that was that.

Now I'm on the way, because I hear what he says to me. And yes, I know he's talking to me. He said, "You have to hear, but also see if you want to come and follow me. So pick up your cross, and remember, I'm master. So pray for attention and hear what I say. Listen closely so you don't lose your way."

CHRIST IN OUR MIDST

I have been given the honor to take up the pen to speak of God, the Father of this one man, his son, our savior and high priest in the life of "Melchizedek." The very name of high honor, for it means, listen, "king of justice." Jesus is also the "king of peace." He remains forever "the beginning and the end." He is high priest forever resembling the son of God!

Consider this, Abraham gave to him a tenth of all he had won in battle over many kings, and the high priest received it and in return gave Abraham (placed upon him) a blessing, the same Abraham, who already had the promises of God (Heb. 6:13). Here is to ponder a thought, the one who receives a blessing is not greater than the one who gives the blessing, as a student is not greater than his teacher, neither was the blessed man of God the father greater than the high priest of the order of Melchizedek as he walked this planet earth as a mere man. Remember Levi was the tribe of the priesthood, given by the laws of Moses.

When the priesthood is changed, as well the law must be changed.

Jesus came from the tribe of Judah, and Moses did not mention Judah in connection with the priesthood.

The change in God's law is evident by the fact that Jesus, the son of God came to earth for the sins of man, to die on the cross, and be resurrected to life again on high on his throne at the right side of God, his Father, forever, by the power of a life that cannot be destroyed.

God took an oath, a promise and will not break the vow.

You are a priest forever in the line of Melchizedek (Heb. 5:5-6).

The old requirement, the law is set aside, into place, the new covenant, Jesus our Lord and savior, the high priest of forever gives life today to those who ask and he gives it "abundantly forever."

The Great Creator, the new covenant for us that he may partake with us (Heb. 8:7-13).

Holy is his name
Lord of love
Amen

Promise Land

It's time to write some of love and light, time to strike out for justice and right, then choke the wrongs and show the Lord's might.

A cry for freedom is heard out in the night, time to free them and see which way to go, some to life on a beam of light, others will fall back in a hole they already know. The ones that choose light, the beam of the sun, the brightness of day, the brilliance of the Lord with his mighty right arm, the stars he holds in his right hand will be like grains of sand all across this land.

Behold, today is the day, the day of the Lord. He stands on high and looks to the sky, gives thanks to his Father for all he gave to you and I, and to defend this land with his mighty sword and all of his might.

Before too long, there will be no darkness in the world, in the middle of the day. The same as no night at the end of the day!

I speak to you as mortal men, take a look and see where you've been. Can you see your path of where you've been and stand up straight to God and say Lord, I am a man, or would you be one that hides in the rock, or digs a hole and says "cover me up, I'm as low as a mole?"

Stop and think just where you've been. For as I said today, yes this day is the day of the Lord. He knows where you've been as well as what you said. Then remember and know this is true; he comes to judge the likes of you. Don't blame your fathers, family, or friends, because he judges them as well.

Truly people, as seen as men, leave the darkness, step into the light, hold your head up, step to the right, take your place with a robe of white and pray to God. Do the best you can. Help the Lord save this land, for it's his gift to the people of his choice, for this is the promise, this land. Pick up your sword and strike out the night.

Praise God, for his son, your Holy Lord and his promise from the beginning, this is the promised Lord. What makes a difference is where you stand.

Amen and Amen

THE WORTH OF DAYS

What is your worth? Do you have low or no self-esteem? Just what is your worth? Are you one that will stand and claim the making of a man? Are you the one who will defend the right of truth right and liberty? Will you stand when no mere man can and say, "I come to fight for my king!" Are you a man that came out of the wilderness that you see? Do you find him weak and dirty like a reed, moved by the breath of the wind, or do you see a man dressed to kill from a castle just over the hill? Or are you looking for a prophet? Yes, and more than a prophet is he, a messenger of the Lord your God that says, "I'm sending my messenger before you, that he may prepare your way before you." I ask again, what is your worth that your Lord Jesus Christ would lay down his own life just to save you, a mere man of clay?

The message was John the Baptist's; out in the wilderness, he shouted out to all who would listen to prepare for the way of the Lord. If you will understand and listen to what I say, you will understand the strength of a man called by God. For from the time John, the Baptist, began preaching and baptizing; the kingdom of heaven has been advancing and violent people oppose it. For all the teachings of the scriptures, look forward to this present time. If you will accept what is said, he, Elijah, the one the prophets said would come.

All who are willing to listen should hear, see, and seek, to understand the Lord of the beginning, the Lord of the end, the alpha and the omega is alive and well today. Lord Jesus sits today on his throne and knows you by name.

What did you say was your worth? Listen, hear what Jesus has to say about the rest of your days and your worth.

Remember, the Christ child lives today and is still the way to the Father.

Wisdom is shown to be right by the results of the day.

Today's Joy

Joy to the world today, the Master of the creation has risen and in heaven recorded his own.

I say again rejoice!

Express yourself in deepest gratitude and joy of heart, that you're Lord and King has come again, to rescue you too himself and give to all, the gift of life just for the asking. I say again, just for the asking, salvation to all whom would live with our Lord Christ Jesus.

The scoreboard of life says Satan lost. The Lord and Christ won and in all of us with the Holy Spirit that believe in him and ask of him for mercy, grace and peace, and make the request with a heart full of humility, that your name has been recorded in the book of life. That you too, have won as you ask Jesus, the risen Christ to come in and share your life.

A word of discernment, count your blessings without the Lord in your life, trouble, strife to name a couple to start the list.

Then count your blessing with the Lord in your life, born again, real life comes your way.

I say again, rejoice, the Lord has come and with him blessings galore, like raindrops from heaven, your blessings will pour. Though he was God, he made himself humble and a servant and slave. He came into the world as a man in human form and later died on the cross a criminal's death on the cross. Then risen by his Father and placed on the throne as the most high, God's son, so that every knee shall bow in heaven and on earth and under the earth.

Every tongue shall confess that Christ Jesus is Lord to the glory of God the Father.

I say again, rejoice with joy and count your blessings, you have been found. Salvation has come. Praise to our brother and Father, thanks to the family of God, the blessings of the way in our Christ and Lord Jesus, the author of the way to salvation and life.

Joy, I heard him say today.

REJOICE TODAY

Let me restate what has been said for nearly three thousand years in the Scripture. Fear not for I Am is with you, worry not about the tomorrow nor fret of yesterday, worry not, can you change one hair on your head or change its color from the inside out. Look to the flowers of the field, a beautiful touch of color and the morrows of life gone, the next only to arise again as next of kin to be beautiful for God again. Fear not, for the Lord our God has stated, "I Am with you always and will never forsake you."

If you look close to the word of God and see the word of God, he says, "Fear not, I have overcome the world. Worry not of your tomorrow, because as I Am with you today, I Am also with your tomorrow and will be there with you as well." He said, "I go to my Father's, house to prepare a place for you, in my Father's house are many rooms. If it were not so I would tell you plainly. "Fear not, I Am here with you. For the Lord your God has arrived to live among you. He is a mighty savior. He will rejoice over you with great gladness.

With his love, he will calm all your fears. He will exult over you by singing a happy song (Zeph. 3:17).

Today, the spirit of God says to your spirit, "Believe and trust the truth of the lord of peace. Today I say rejoice, joy to the world, for I have overcome and my people by my word will overcome. Ask, it will be given what so ever you ask in my name, will be done for you. Rejoice!"

Again I say, "Trust in the lord of truth and follow the way of his path."

Rejoice, for he knows your name and will proclaim it to God, his Father, and his angels that you are his and that he saved from the pits of hell. Yes, rejoice the Lord's day today! That's what I heard him say today. Rejoice (Phil. 4:4)!

Look Up

Here I Am, I want to play today. The Holy Spirit is upon you, so listen. Hear what he has to say. Speak truth of any kind, but seek your truth from your God's Holy Book, so that you may not be lead astray. Listen to what I say, for I tell only what I'm told to say.

The ascension of Jesus had to come to fulfill God's plan to send the Holy Spirit to the people of his plan, that I pray, come to every man as I teach them the secret of God's great plans for man. Let me say here not to misplace a thought, God's plan includes everyone down to the very last man and keep the souls from the fires of hell.

When you seek to be a star, remember, just who you are. Talk to God up high above and let him give you a touch of his love. For no mortal man can be more than they be, for God makes the stars you see. Jesus said, "I hope you get to be all that you can ever hope to be, for I hold the stars in my hand, you see." He also said, "I Am the bright morning star that takes the darkness out of a bright knight and showers him with love of my Father from above. I make the stars and all you will ever see, come follow me. You will plainly see the stars are made in my father's house to shine brightly in the light for all to see. My father makes mortal men out of clay. Lord Jesus gives them the light of the stars that you see in them.

Today, that's what the spirit of God said to me. "Look," he said to me, "just what did you expect to see, when you ask to be just like me. A star I make of thee." Shine brightly, the light of love your Father gave to you and me. Jesus said, "My Father and I are one."

As the grains of sand, the stars of heaven you shall plainly see. "Watch the bright morning star," Jesus said to me.

"I Am he," he said to me, "look up for the love of God. Do this for me, look up."

Those, who become Christians, become new, the old is gone, a new life begins (2 Cor. 5:17)!

FRIEND OF CHRISTMAS

No matter how much we struggle, no matter what trouble comes to call, better to stand for Lord Jesus than never stand at all. Only in his light do we have the right, only with his mighty arm do we stand or fall.

Only with God's love do we learn to bend, for without, we'd be ridged and break with the pressure of life's great storm.

The spirit of God is in the air; the spirit of Christ I smell this day. Remember, he is known as the living Christmas tree. Yet stood high on the cross, at Calvary! To give life to all people that could see and hear the son of God, as he rang the bell of eternity. Through the ages, all that believed in the son of God. As the son of man, might have everlasting life to hear the call of life and shout with glee, "The Lord picked me, the Lord picked me." What an honor, for the Scripture says, "I know whom I have chosen to follow and to lead the stray, come follow me. I will show you the way, for my Father and I are alive and well, to this very day."

Holy, holy, holy is the Lord God almighty, the one who is, the one who was, and the one who is still to come.

As you live and breathe this day, look for your blessings of God almighty, for today, his spirit has come close to you, as you read I say, "The heavenly kingdom of God is right near, waiting for you to knock and open the door. It's up to you to choose to hear and see the things of God, his son, Jesus. Follow as he leads the way. Believe, believe in me. Ask, I will give myself to you, the love of God this very day."

All of us need to find God, seek his son. To lead the way one and the same is what I heard my spirit say. Be a light on the living Christmas tree that shines brightly every single living day.

Path of a Friend

Time to write to you my friend of things I see written in the sky. The winds of winter I see are setting in. It's a long time to come before the Fourth of July. For the chilling cold will soon enter in, and life and limb in peril, will men soon be out in the weather and wind where men can't see or make claim to be more than they be.

For it's time to pray to God, winter in the sky that I see a man and his dog walking a path they can't see the warmth of house and family again. They hope to see, knowing the treachery of the darkness and the dangers that want for thee. They wait on the weather in a hollow and huddle together for warmth, knowing they've only a short way to go, but it is cold out in that driven blinding snow. They huddle and wait for what they do not know. They cannot make it home alone in the driven, howling, freezing snow.

Then a light appeared, an angel they thought it to be, then a soft voice said, "Behold, fear not, the Lord has heard your prayer and has come to share his light with thee."

I Am the morning star, I dance and tingle with pure delight when I hear an earnest prayer in a cold winter's night, knowing the evils of darkness lay in wait, hoping a good person they can catch in their snares, hoping they will forget to say a prayer. But the Lord has come to shed his light on the earthly scum that in evil, take their delight, for the Lord Jesus is watching and listens to those lost and forlorn, with no hope of being found, that say a prayer to God above (Ps. 34:15).

He comes forth quickly in the darkness of night. And with great force and vengeance, his crash of thunder, the arc of his great light, the night is gone, the evil on the run, a new day shining, a brand new song; the Lord has answered.

You have only to ask, to be a beam of his light. Call on Lord Jesus. He will come to take you on home (Ps. 32:8-10).

The Path of a Friend

MASTER PLAN WONDERLAND

To be fruitful in this world, we're passing through. We must have a glad heart, a stout mind with a memory of Christ in our heart and all the gifts he gives. We only have to ask of him as we have a need to use his blessings. As we pass them along to the poor and needy and tell them how this is part of God's plan, that we may spread his word all across this great land. He calls the promise land America the beautiful, the gracious skies, the land of the wonder and whys. Think of this great land, think of this world, think as a great man, (or woman), as the case maybe.

What do we contribute to the God of the what? Everything that ever was and the God of all that will ever be! The thinking is getting deeper, come up for air, take a breath too. Ask to receive if we believe, love to love, love to be loved. Christ said, "My peace I give to you. My love I give to you. My joy I also give to you. I give that you may give also as well. For whoever handles well the little that he has, will be given more abundantly, to give as well." The Lord's people have the warehouse full of the Lord's fruits to disburse. We only have to ask. Yes, just ask and wait on the Lord to show the way to disburse his love or whatever he deems for you to give. Remember, its God's plan to be worked, not our own. Give yourself to him completely and watch a small miracle happen before your very eyes as he works his plan for your life as he guides you to others that you may guide them to him.

Please stop and think, this very day, the Christ your Lord wants you in his army and in his master plan.

The amazing grace of God! His son and the gift! I Am he, he said to me, and I welcome those I choose, the ones that see what they hear. I judge the quick as well as the dead. I Am the spirit of the Lord, my truth you shall see.

Friend and Provider

SPIRIT OF THE WAY

Tell me just what is it that you hear when the spirit speaks to you? Do you stop and pay attention, do you tremble in fear? Just what is it that you hear?

Do you fear the Lord, and try to hide or just pay no mind? Or say I'm busy and speak to me some other time? Do you ask, "Just what did you say?" Answer me quickly before you go away. Truly, I would like to know what you heard as I spoke to you this day. Did you kneel down and humbly pray, "Father who art in heaven hallowed be thy name, thy kingdom comes." Just what did you think you heard me say, when I touched you and said, "Child, I love you." Let me show you the way. Trust in the one true God, the one that loves you no matter what. Trust in the only God that can help you in this world you're passing through. Trust in his son, the Lord Christ Jesus, the one that came and died and came again for you to claim and save from hell and take your many sins all away.

Thank God for his son. Thank Jesus that cares for us, who sees all we do. Who knows all we do and can still love us for the good of our very soul! Yes, thank God for his love. Thank Jesus, that he died for our love and thank the Holy Spirit that bring us his love even to this very day. Then remember today is the Lord's, day when he said, "I love you child." What did you think you heard him say?

Who cares? The spirit cares and would like to help you as you come along the way. One thing that Jesus asks of me is that I lean on him, that I put my complete trust in him, that I surrender myself completely, that he will be my guide. I pray that the Holy Spirit fill you with his purity, that he takes all that is impure, that you may find and know this God we call Lord and love, that you each one of you may live in the spirit of God.

The Lord said, "My Father and I are one. The Holy Spirit I send to you, that you may come. The dinner bell has rung. I Am the only one, come child, come run."

I heard him say today. What did you hear him say?

I thank God, I heard him say.

The Love of a Friend

SHEPHERD'S LIGHT

A time to love, a time to share! A time to give, a time to care!

Love your neighbor, make sure he sees himself. Make a friend. Shake a hand as you travel this land. Take a trip, this is the promise land. Take the time and see what you can see.

Have fun, entertain people, be as nice as you can be and keep your eyes open, an angel you might see.

Be a spirit sent from God, spread his message, show his love. Stand up tell the world, if it's not of light, then it's wrong. For all made in darkness and shadow of the night can only show wrong with the coming of light, be a person of the day. Remember, Jesus said, "I Am, the way. Today, anyone who hears my calling or sees my light, take refuge with me. Drop your heavy burdens, and I'll make your yoke light."

Stand as a beacon as you flash your light and watch darkness disappear with the coming of light. Into the darkness the beams of light go. Who will see the light spread out in the night, the lost ones of the shepherd, the lost sheep I suppose. For they, will come running with glee. Once they see the light they will come and say, "I'm lost," then the shepherd will say, "You are not lost child, you have been found, follow me. I will lead your way." The day will come when you will hear the Lord say to his Father and the angels of heaven, "These are mine, I found along the way and saved from hell."

This is the story, he said to tell, that he came to save, to heal, to lead, to his Father's house those that hear and see. So do you hear what you see?

I *Am he, he* said to me. Jesus, Lord of Light.

Amen

A Stone's Throw

Impeachment is the word that has spread across this land, but is impeachment the word of God. What does he say with the language of his hand, truth, honor, and justice!

Just who threw the first stone? Just who would break your bones? The love of God! Blame the sin, not the man. He was placed by God to govern this great land and by the grace of God. He will know that he has done wrong. Don't let evil get the best of you. Conquer evil by doing very good. As you know is right in God's sight. For it is written in the Scripture: "I will take vengeance, I will repay those who deserve it," says the Lord.

Instead, do what the scriptures say, and if you feed your enemies when they are hungry and give them drink, they will be ashamed of what they have done to you (Lev. 19:18).

As surely as I live, says the Lord, every knee shall bow to me and every tongue will confess allegiance to God (Isa. 49:18).

So why do you condemn other Christians? Why do you look down on them? Remember, each of us must stand personally before the judgment seat of God.

Yes, each of us will have to give a full personal account to God. Let us quit trying to do God's work for him and let the Holy Spirit of God do the work that is to be done through him, by him, for the glory of God and the humble honor of man, the respected gentlemen of the House of Representatives and the members of Congress must look at the stone in their hands as well also at the rock in their heart.

God bless this great land! Again remember, the president is just a man. It's easy to replace a man. It's evil that has spread across this land, with the lust, greed, and corruption that mortal man has spread across this land, the ones that forgot God and said with greatness in their heart, "I am a self-made man."

The Lord said to say, "Now it's time for my father and I."

The spirit writes what it wants to say. I merely dot the, i's along life's way.

That's what he said to say today.

A Friend

I am Lives

Here I Am, this day on earth to tell all man, of my cause and my worth. I Am all that you will ever see. I Am also all that you can ever hope to be.

I Am, the light you see in the sky, known to man as the bright morning star. I hold all man's thoughts in the palm of my hand. I hear man sing all across the land. I also hear the sorrow that the night and darkness bring. I lay claim to those I call my own. I also write the book. I call the book of atone.

I give life to those who call my name. I give direction to those I choose to claim.

I Am the Christ, as a man, all mankind could ever hope to be. As a friend, take the time to count to three. I Am, before the apple and the tree. I Am, today, as well you can plainly see.

I Am, the spirit of love, which my Father made of me. To spread his grace for all, the world to see, "believe" and you will surely see life, love, and eternity; one, two, three; it's so easy to get a glimpse of me. Again, on the count of three, I Am, I was and forever, I Am to always be.

I give joy to the world, hope to the heart, life to the living. As well as living, love and to those who ask in my name of my father, I will know them by name as marked in the book of life, and they will have salvation to the ends of eternity, and they shall never die in vain but have life eternal. My word is truth which makes it true.

It is said in the Scripture, God so loved the world that he gave his only begotten son, to die for the likes of you and I, then raised him on the third day.

The cry I put across the sky is "I Am" alive and well. Believe, believe I Am he of whom he said "I Am." Believe, be all that you can be. See, I Am he, and if you ask, you can live with me. Read the holy word, learn of my Father and me,

Come, take my hand. Ask and receive. Believe I Am he, he said to me. Spread this word with the wind, the word and love I give to thee.

A Friend

HIS PROMISE TRUE

I ask my God for blessings and all good things that I thought might help in my mind as I walked the garden. Taking my walk, when I heard him say in a matter-of-fact kind of way, we have already walked that walk. Remember back and bring to mind when you ask for strength that you might achieve. I made you weak that you learn to obey. When you ask for good health to do great things I gave you that infirmity that you might do greater things or that time you wanted a tune to hum, I gave you a song that you could sing.

You ask for all things that you might enjoy life, so I gave you, life. I made you weak that you would feel the need of your God, then, gave you time and space so that you would remember your place.

You ask for all good things to make you feel blessed. I gave you my son, that he might take your place. That with him you would learn to grow, that with him you would know love, my love, sent from above on the wings of a dove.

Remember, John witnessed this out in the river in the wilderness. My promise is true, if you have my son, my love lives with you.

Draw close to God, feel his son, walk his walk as he walks with you, for time and space is simply a place that God gives to you!

He has said in the Scriptures, "In the beginning, I Am."

He has said in the Scriptures I will never leave you. His promise is true. Again John witnessed this. John 3:16: For God so loved the world he gave his only begotten son, so that everyone who believes in him will not perish but have eternal life.

So please remember when you're feeling down and feel it's hard to get your nose off the ground, think bright, turn on your light, "look up," give thanks and say a prayer, this promise is true he will do for you.

I Am said to say to you today, "His promise will always be true."

WALK THE LAND OF I AM

Let me speak this day of the land of God known as the land of I Am. His Holy Son, in whom he is well pleased.

Let me praise and thank the Father this day for the "gift" of his son, the bright morning star, that beam of light, that says, "I Am the one," that says, "I Am before the world." I am before time began. Let me speak of light, when you magnify the light, you see the son. My Father and I are one. All that is or ever will be belongs to the son, My Father gave this all to me and then made him the high priest in all holy righteousness of the past, the present and the all that will ever be.

In the light of truth, I Am. In the light and life, a man I Am. In the light of spirit, I am he of whom he said I Am. My family is those that hear and see and do the will of my Father as my Father goes, so is the way of the son. Yes, this is the promise land, the land of the great I Am, the holy of holies, the beam of light that shines all across this land and strikes out at darkness in the middle of the night to declare a way with you, all who are not true, the ones that like the darkness and try to hide from the light. The Lord knows who he's talking to. Is he talking to you? This is the time of the Lord, this is the time he will judge and say, "Who goes and who stays." For only his people will he allow to stay and only by grace will some find their way.

Yes, let me say it this way, only will be, in the land of I Am, only doing the will of God led by his son will any be allowed to stay in God, the son, family, the ones that do (see and hear) the will of God, it's in the Scripture, read the word, accept the son, lord of the light. Pray to God, you may follow the son. Walk out of the desert, come into his light. John said, "Prepare ye the way of the Lord" (John 3:3).

I say today is the day of the Lord. I say he is here with his baptism of the Holy Spirit or the pits of hell, for those that rebel, the time is very near, in fact it is here. Matthew spoke of John in his time, speaking of future events, these times now. We walk the path to heaven or the path to the fires of hell. Jesus judges, but the choice is yours (Matt. 3:11-12, Mark 9:48, Isaiah 66:24).

Jesus says it very clear: "None can come to the Father except through me, my way is the only path to life."

LETTER FROM A FRIEND

A note to say Jesus cares in every little way, no matter what you do or say, all you will ever hear him say, will always say "Child, I love you" each and every day. I have walked with him from the cross through the sand. I have followed his great salvation plan. I have the faith, I have the hope. Oh yes, I have his love.

I have had the honor to see his truth, also to take his hand. I Am he, he said to me. Write this of light, an never-ending flame that will always burn in your heart, a fountain of living water, called life, a vessel of skin is all we can ever offer him. Yet he is pleased with everyone he sees as they walk his plan. Remember, he's talking to you and loves to give those little delights. Look for them make it a habit to seek out his love. He will amaze you. See, now you know, God does really have a plan. Truth is a light for all to see. Whether a candle for a fallen comrade, or a beacon by the sea. Light and truth are to be seen, that's why the lord of lights message has always been and will always be, come and follow me.

My Father loves to give to those that see his light. For then he knows they are his.

Again remember, once was said, "I have a dream;" a black man once said that. For holding up that truth, he was shot by an assassin's gun. The Lord is the maker of dreams, his kingdom comes.

I have picked up his sword of light, truth, and honor; I use as the shield of armor of God. I wear the protective cover of his love, his quest.

To put it plainly, I have come to fight for my king and declare his love to you. I say again, his kingdom comes.

Amen, Love

LIGHT OF DAY

In the light of day, the sun sets at the end of its time. Again it rises at the start of a new day in the light as it takes a new day out of the morrows of time as the old one is slid into the past of yesterday. Time never again to beckon its day again, except in remembrance of time well spent. With the Lord, we have a draw of springs and things or wills of the well, I tell of these things that are here around us but not seen by some. For with the God of creation and his living son, we have rocks that can cry out, also rocks that can spring forth water so the Scriptures do tell. For with God, all things are possible (Matt 11:28-30).

Jesus said, "Come to me, all of you who are weary and carry heavy burdens, I will give you rest. Take my yoke upon you. Let me teach you, because I Am humble and gentle, and you will find rest for your souls. For my yoke fits perfectly, and the burden I give you is light." The promise of Jesus is the power of light, and the power of light is God's truth, light over darkness. Truth stands the test of time, lies fail every time when exposed to light and tried with truth, the night turns to light and again we see the light of Jesus standing, the bright morning *star* (Rev 22:16).

So I say to you this day, take hold of the sword of light that the Lord has offered you. Give your praise and thanks for your days and give out with the Lord's battle cry.

Joy to the world, my peace I give to you. Not the world's peace, but my peace I give to you. The light of day, the light of life, and the promise of true life for eternity, the light of God, is the light of truth.

He said to ask, "Where do you get your light tonight, if not from his son each day?"

The bright morning star, the light of day, lives today . . . (Rev. 22:16)!

Jesus said, "I Am the bright morning star, I Am both the source and the heir to his throne."

He said to give this message to those who would listen. The message is free, pray for the answer.

Truth Hurts

Is it because of all this evil that help is far from us?

Is that why God doesn't punish those who do us harm? No wonder we grope around in the darkness when we thought we'd be in the light. No wonder we are like blind people and stumble along. Even in the bright of day and think the Lord has failed us and gave us the darkness and the night as thou he doesn't know us and just doesn't care and we drop into despair (Isaiah 59:13).

A lesson appears in the air, a statement I see. This is what was said to me. Ambition can become that which Satan uses to lure us away from God to destruction. The devil said, "If you will only kneel down and worship me, I will give it all to you" (Matt 4:8-10).

Then the word said, "You must worship only the Lord your God. Serve him."

Then a dove landed in my ear and a promise from God, I did hear.

Feed the hungry, help those in need. Then your light will shine out from the darkness and the darkness around you will be as bright as the day (Isaiah 58:10-11). The Lord will guide the way. Believe—Ask—Receive. That's what was said to me.

The spirit of the Lord is upon me and appointed me to tell of the good news to the poor. To comfort the broken-hearted. To announce prisoners will be freed.

He has sent me to tell all who mourn. The time of the Lord's favor has come (Acts 1:8).

To say boldly as never before, believe of God. Followers of our Lord Christ Jesus, strength and guidance come with the light according to the anointing of the Holy Spirit.

Believe, ask, accept and receive. Believe I Am he, he said to me.

Brings a thought to mind, when you are at the bottom of the pit, all hope is gone. Try looking up, help is in the sky. Praise the Lord, "thank God" (Jer. 38:13).

Have faith, the brothers and sisters send you God's love.

Amen

Hear, am I, Friend

I HEARD HIM SAY

Love your neighbor as yourself, goodwill toward men.
Speak truth and be true to yourself.
That's the high calling of God, our Lord and savior, that's the very working of his plan for mortal man that we do work his plan. Look around you, what is it you see in the land—mass corruption, lust, and greed? I want that, give it to me! Is that what you see?

President Kennedy got a glimpse when he said don't ask what your country can do for you, but what you can do for your country.

On a higher note, what about God? What about his love that he has given to those who live here? The son that died on the cross for the sins of all mankind, that's personal. He died for you, and he died for me. Open your eyes. God forgave us because of his love for man, his creation that we could live and breathe that we could love you, him and me.

I am your friend even if you can't see me. I was sent from God, my name is love. I also give joy and peace to name just a few of the things I give to you. Take a look around, I give you, life that you may stand upon the ground and breathe the air, because I care.

Martin Luther King said, "I have a dream." Just what was it that man seen? Do you think it possible, I gave him a glimpse of a thought I had already seen?

The song is true as I have for you, goodwill toward men.

That's what he said to say. He said to understand his word. Ask for his wisdom. Be aware that he is here with you and me. Time is here that we should hear and turn to him and see that he's the one that calls out, come follow me.

God is with you, he said to me. Tell your friends you speak for me.

A Friend

QUESTIONS ANSWERED

If I could pour out my heart to you, say I'm sorry and make a brand new start, what could I say that would make my life worthy of forgiveness and granting of your love, the dove of your grace and your never-ending love!

What could I do to earn the robe and the ring of your love, the life ring that has no end!

I know I can never earn the right, yet by your strength I can accept your light, I can stand in your light and expect the judgment of my Lord, to my dying day or accept pardon to the path to life, the way of truth, The love of love, the surrender to my God, the gift of life, and the way to the path this day. Forgive them Father. They know not what they do. Does this ring a bell? Is this the truth, to tell the people of the garden, the ones that the Lord, my God, can save from hell?

I ask you again, do you hear this crystal bell that says come, sup with me here in my Father's house. Please don't say I wish I could come before it's too late and the gatekeeper comes and closes the gate. For this bell rings for the sick and tired sinners of this world. Not for the ones whom think they are well enough or good enough (Rom. 4:14). The road to hell is wide. Only the chosen ones of God can know the way of the narrow path, the only true way.

It's with my heart and my love that I search for my people that have lost their way. It's with my strong right arm I offer my hand to all mine that hear my calling "come, be found;" again, I say come follow me, take my hand, I will show you the way to my Father's house where his people live and play and listen to my Father. Tell the story of mere men, "mortals." I heard him say that he loves to make out of bone, spices, and clay.

The son of man shook my hand; this day, he said write this down, I'll tell you what to say. I looked at my hand; a ballpoint pen in my hand did lie. He said, "I Am the way, today." Then he added, "Every teacher of religious law, who has become a disciple in the kingdom of heaven is like a person who brings out of the storehouse the new teaching as well as the old" (Matt. 13:52).

PS. Again, I heard him say, *I am he*, of whom he said *I Am*.

SON OF THE SON

If I had not to do this day, would I call on my Lord and pray. Would I praise him as I should for doing what he promised he would?

If I had not a dime, could I really take the time to get on my knees and give him praise for all he's given me?

Well, believe me when I say for God's truth I speak this day. I'm a son of the son, and with his sword, Christ, my Lord, has this day knighted me in the way with his word just because I ask him.

I was on my knees with a prayer for thee. Of safety in this realm, when somewhere I was there, kneeling from time everlasting, in front of him, when he said, "Stand for truth, with all my might, kneel for blessings and honor. Stand strong and true." I say to you. You're a warrior made of clay. The truth you speak, most people seek; only he know, where and when to find them, but only if and when they ask of him. He's very bold, all covered with gold, my Lord of everlasting, and what I can say, I've been told in truth today. Everlasting is here for those who can hear and seeks those that ask him. He said, "Be clear, the time is very near." He said, "To come in fear." On this I'm not quite clear, but he did say to come in fear.

He said to be true when I spoke to you and to tell that you must ask him.

I'm a son of the son, a real son of the one, and this day I've come to everlasting.

I'm a son of the son, a new life I've begun. Yes, a life everlasting. I got it with a grin, just by asking of him. As I said before, just knock on his door and when he opens, just ask of him. Then you too can be a son of the son everlasting!

Did I say if I had to do today, the son I'd just bask in? So if you're all alone, come on home I'm here to say the Lord is the way, today.

He said, "He is the way, today. If you don't believe in me and what I say, why don't you just ask."

In all you say and do, remember what I told you, I'm just a son in the light of the one we know is to come. I say again, "all you have to do is ask him."

A LOVE LIGHT

I see the light. I see the light, no more darkness, no more fright, an old song but the same light. Two thousand years and it is still shining bright.

Let's look closely at this bright spot of white light. To some, it's a candle lit in a prayer for someone. To ships at sea, it's a beacon they can see, to let them pass safely and miss unseen treachery. Let's look closely, not only is it a prayer light or a great ship's beacon it's also a love light you see in the eyes. It's a light of relief, a light to despair, it's a light to sorrow and in a time of need, it's the light of the world. And yes even more, it's the light of the bright morning star. It's a wonder unto its self, a miracle by name that only the Lord can claim.

It's a fire that glows in the night. It's a candle in the window or a castle on a hill shining in the night. Let's think of this power, might, truth, and justice. Loyalty and honor for these make up the light.

God will never burn you, trust the light.

Jesus

Jesus, if you have a need,
I have a need, too.
If you have a want,
I want, too.

If you have a cause,
Make it my, cause as well.

If you have water to flow,
Let me help make it glow.

If you have a life,
I can live, too.

To sum it up,
I want to live for you.

If you ask what
Do you want?
I would just say,
I want to do it with you.

AMEN

PRAISE GOD

You, did you praise God today?
As you sharpened your sword?

You, did you thank the Lord
When he told you what to say today?

Did you stop to pray awhile?
You helped your friend?

Do you love to do what?
He wants for you?

Do you sing a hymn or
Whistle a tune as you go,
Merrily on your way!

He may be out of place
With this human race,
But just remember, you get your grace
From him!

FATHER

It's time to try to say,
Thanks for all you have done
For this man,
You call son.
I mean to say things
That I feel for you
Thou the time flies by,
And things get put
On the run!
I'd like to express
How much I care
And say thanks for
All the times that
You were there.
Feelings of love
Seem so hard
To compare,
Now that you are gone,
Not forgotten.

AMEN

LOVE

Do you love to live!
Do you live to love!
Do you try to live!
Not knowing why

Life is a gift
Given of God
Not knowing where
You came from
Not knowing where!
You have been

A fresh start
Beginning life anew
Once you begin to be
Just like him

GOD'S SONG

The finger of God
Points the way every day to
His son and our Lord Jesus!

Still we tend to lose our way
To this very day!
We once a day
At the start of our day
Walk away from the right way.

The way of our Lord,
As we search for our own
Wisdom to light the dawn!

Thanks be given
To God, that he
Gave his only son
That we may find him!

That he died for us,
That, we one day
Might find and hear
His song!

BELIEVE AND SEE

We all think we can,
But can we really see?
Until Jesus says,
Your sins are forgiven,
Your faith has made you well,
Open your eyes,
For now you may see,
The kingdom of my Father
As I show you the way
Hear and see
Know I Am he,
Said he to me!
Believe!

LOST SHEEP
CHILDREN OF GOD

(Found of Him)

They come from the dark of the night. Scared, lame, helpless, meek, and be withered to touch and feel the grace of love from that eternal bright light JESUS, knowing only vast darkness, crippled from falling with nothing to hand on too but terror and fright. They come without knowing even where they have been. Never knowing his love or things as they might have been. But today, this day I Am, seen them and gave of his light, that they may warm their minds and bodies and see the truth and warmth of his guiding light. No matter where they've wandered, lost and alone. They may find grace and wonder and light to find their way home. Never let it be said that I Am is at home alone. Bright is the night when the Lord turns on the light.

Three thoughts on light and darkness!

1. *In the light of thirty silver coins one truth walked away. Darkness got none.*
2. *In the light of truth, there's no darkness, not one.*
3. *The best way to hide a truth is between two lies. See which one stands out and turns on the light? One thought on life, TRUTH.*

The record of new birth has none except God. (BORN AGAIN)

I Am the way, the truth and the life. Man says! "Give me liberty or give me death."

The Christ of I Am says, "Give even your life that I may overcome your death. Life eternal for those who come with me! I Am, the gift and the prize. Those who can hear open your eyes."

MAN FROM HEAVEN

Who's the man from heaven?
Christ Jesus is his name.
Who's the man from heaven?
Lord Jesus, one and the same!
What do you think he's doing?
What do you think of his game!
Who's the man from heaven?
Jesus and I'll tell you of his name.
He died for all us sinners.
He crucified our blame.
He died for all his people.
Took their pain and shame!
Who's the man from heaven?
That takes away our shame.
His name is Holy Jesus.
Saving grace is his game.
What do you think of Jesus?
What do you think his game?
Just come and ask forgiveness
And follow in his name.

He'll give you, life eternal.
Just ask in Jesus's name.
There's treasure in his promise.
There's profit in his claim.
Give your life to Jesus.
He'll give you everything, life.
Who's this man from heaven?
A lion you can tame.
He's the lamb of life eternal.
Forever, just the same!
So give your life to Jesus.
He's the man from heaven.
A brother just the same!
Come and drink his water.
Remember, in his claim.
Life eternal!

LORD JESUS, THE MAN

In any language, in any heart in any mind-set, or thought!

For soul or angel beings or human effort cannot bring a more profound thought to the eyes of man or beast on this earth or in heaven, or any concept known to man, than the proficiently of the perfection of the Christ Jesus and his love in his walk as a man on this planet earth, giving praise to his heavenly Father, for all that he was to do, and did it so well, that the wise nor the public recognized him in his humility for humanity out of pure Love to make man as right with his Father that they may be forgiven by the promise of the covenant with his holy son, the Christ Jesus, or Lord and savior of all humanity . . .

For with the Lord Jesus also came the bridge to span the deep cleavage of sin to forgiveness to allow the adoption of man into the house and family of God as sons and daughters of eternal life . . .

Praise God for his everlasting gift!

AMEN, AMEN

A LIFETIME COMMITMENT

The Christ Child
Jesus
Come into my life

Commit to Christ and die

A cross on a hill
A mountain to call home
A child lost come home
With one word, Father! (ABBA)
In the light of darkness, there was
Only light
Jesus
Not one was lost to darkness, except
The son of light was found.
Darkness cannot stand in the
Rays of the son, the only son
In two, stands darkness
Divided
As light in the night darkness was
Naught to be found, only the light
Of God! Our Lord, the son,
Son light everlasting
A bright morning star, a silver moon
Shinning leaves no room for darkness
Only light with a silver lining
Praise God, praise the Lord our God.
Praise the Lord.
I am

LORD JESUS

To do your walk and to do your talk
Let us watch the sun.
As we close the day, remind us to pray,
That I walked your walk and I did
Your talk
And that I did your will this day.
Thank You, Lord Jesus.
Help me in this I pray.
Help me in this I pray,

The Lord Spoke

Pray in the will and love of God and in faith that he will by his grace to you, do his word as he said he would.

In his mercy to his own he will, his will, he will be true, absolutely, faithful totally truthful and all powerful.

The Father of your life, the Lord of your life, as well as the director of your life, when you surrender to his will.

JESUS, asks, who do they say I Am? They answered, ISAIAH, some a PROPHET or the Messiah, then he said, "Whom do you say I Am?"

They said, the God of the creation, the creator of all things seen and all things unseen . . .

The maker of the past, present, and of the future, and the LORD of our live! The one who lives, the one who died, and the one who lives; then he said, I AM HE, of whom he said, I AM, with the mission of Salvation, for those who will believe in my Father whom sent me to save the world. I have the keys of death and the grave, for if you believe in me, you will know my Father as well, and have life eternal, through the son.

Ask, it will be given to you, your needs will be met. Knock, it will be opened for you, look you will find . . .

To those who use well, what is give! More will be in abundance. All is possible to those who believe . . .

The spirit of the LORD has appointed me to tell of the good news, to the poor and the needy . . .

He has sent me to proclaim to the blind that they may see. That the downtrodden may be freed from their oppressors!

The time of the LORD's favor has this day come to thee, believe and receive, give and you will receive in abundance and plenty. I must speak the good news of the kingdom in other places as well, that is why I was sent . . .

I have come to help the sinners turn away from sin. Not to spend or waste my time with those who think they are good enough already.

The LORD speaks, I respond . . . !

Amen.

CHRISTIAN WHO?

What kind are you, the kind that says Christian who? Or are you a Christian today. Do you bother to pray? Or are you one that says, "I'm too busy. I'm having fun . . ."

Do you bother to open the good book to see what it might say? Or shove it to the side, and go out to play.

I really want to ask, how much grace have you used, today. Or how hard did you bother to pray for that other guy? Jesus made it very clear, unproductive spirituality, will soon simply pass away. So my friend, listen to your heart, try and find the beat and try to do your part! In all you do, think or say, try to do for others, as you would have them do for you. But in all you do, please keep in mind you need to find the time. Then put it to use and pray . . .

Remember my friend, Christian is not just in a name, but in fact it's the daily things you do. A way of life free of worry and strife; that's the reason my man, Jesus, calls you his friend, is walking in his way of life.

The Bible is true to you, it will mold a man, one of sand, maybe a little clay. One that can stand if any man can! Jesus's promises are true, and he says he will stand with you. See marriage is two that stand as one spirit a light that spans the times. Love is truth and honor as it stands in the very presence of God, see the Christian lays down the life of sin so God can give him new life that he may live again as freeman without bad habits and sin, serving the Lord Jesus, and that you can truly say, my Lord and Savior live with me today . . .

So I ask you again my friend, your name was
        CHRISTIAN WHO . . . ?

THE TIME OF SORROWS BEGINS

Have you ever looked around, being afraid of being alone, or the hair on the back of your neck bristle and not know why?

Ever walk home alone at night, through dark streets, or alleys and have the feeling you are being followed, or fear that someone will reach out and grab you?

Ever wish that some nice good guy would come along with a flashlight, maybe humming a little tune, fear not the time is near, the evil ones will run, the darkness, will disappear, the good guys are coming, in fact some are already here . . . They have bright lights to flash in the night. The light is so bright it's not even night; now that's a flash of light, with the joy light and laughter the dark times will disappear. The good people will be people of the Lord. Yes, they will be there to help you find your way home.

Yes, open your eyes to Jesus. Ask him to take you home. He has time for everyone, but watch, the evil ones run. It's no fun, if Jesus, puts the fear of God in them, and lights the darkness. No place to hide. They have only lust, greed and foolish pride. So my advice to you my friend, is ask the Lord into your life, and drink his cup of cheer, ask him before he closes the gates. Then won't let you in . . .

They will stand outside and wail and moan and say "Jesus, let us in;" he will say "away with you, I'm not of you," and not let them in. It's a sad story, if you have not his glory to open your heart and do your part, to merrily ask him in and drink of his cup, salvation and good cheer . . . Knowing he was standing right here . . . This is a true story, I speak of mortal men. They choose to wait until it's too late buried in their sin, that won't get to enter in . . .

THE TIME OF SORROWS BEGINS!

LIGHT IN THE NIGHT

THE PICTURE IS CLOUDY, I CAN'T SEE IT REAL CLEAR, BUT I CAN HEAR THE CRY, WAY UP IN THE SKY, THAT SAY'S HIS TIME IS NEAR I HEAR A VOICE NOT OF CHOICE, THAT AT TIMES I CAN HEAR QUITE CLEAR, IT SAYS THE TIME HAS COME FOR SOME, BUT WAIT, IT'S NOT TO LATE FOR SOME, I SEE A LIGHT SHINING, OUT IN THE DARK OF NIGHT, IT'S NOT TO DIM BUT KIND OF GRIM AND QUITE HARD TO SEE, NOW I CAN SEE HE'S WAVING TO ME, AND HIS LIGHT GOT BRIGHT, OUT IN THE NIGHT FOR NOW I CAN SEE PLAINLY IT'S THE LORD DOWN BY THE FIORD AND HE'S CALLING TO YOU AND ME, HE'S ACROSS THE FIORD, MY DEAR, LORD, YES I CAN HEAR HIM SAY TO YOU AND ME, IT'S TIME TO COME AND BE FRUITS OF LIFE, UPON HIS LIVING, LIGHTED CHRISTMAS TREE.

WHEN HE SAID THIS I WAS IN PURE BLISS, JUST TO THINK HE WAS TALKING TO ME.

HE SAID TAKE TWO BOARDS TO CROSS THE FIORD AND COME AND FOLLOW ME, FOR AS YOU CAN PLAINLY SEE, IT'S ME ALIVE, AND YOU BELONG TO ME!

IT'S THE TIME FOR ALL MAN KIND TO LEAVE THE STREETS OF HELL SO TAKE THE CALL AND GO TELL ALL, THE LORD SAID THEIR VERY LIVES DEPENDS ON ME . . .

THE FIORD'S A BODY OF WATER AND A CREVICE YOU CAN PLAINLY SEE, SO TELL EACH MAN OUT IN THE LAND TO TAKE THE BOARDS TO THE FIORD, TAKE HIS CROSS AND COME AND FOLLOW ME, FOR YOU WILL NOT GET LOST, IF YOU USE THE CROSS, FOR HE HAS CROSSED THE FIORD FOR THEE . . .

I'VE BEEN TOLD THAT IF I'M BOLD, I CAN HOLD THE LIGHT, KEEP OUT THE NIGHT SO HE WON'T CLOSE THE GATE ON THIS LAND.

FOR HE ALREADY SAID HE'D NOT LEAVE US FOR DEAD, IF WE'D JUST TAKE HIS OUTSTRETCHED HAND!

SO PICK UP YOUR CROSS, ALL IS NOT LOST, FOR THE LIKES OF YOU AND ME, SO PLEDGE YOUR SWORD, ONLY TO THE LORD, AND A TOUCH OF HEAVEN YOU'LL QUICKLY SEE, GOD, THE LORD, AND ME.

ETERNAL LIGHT AND LIFE, HE PROMISED ON LIFE'S CHRISTMAS TREE, JOY TO THE WORLD, IS WHAT HE SAID TO ME, I AM HE, SAID HE TO ME . . . The joy of the Christmas tree is what he gave to me, Amen.

THE GREAT LIGHT FLASH

As the glory unfolds, this is as I've been told. I have only this light to defend me.

So I pick up this light and shine into the night.

I'm a fisher of men, so you must know where I've been, out in the night with my trusty old light for I learned long ago to flash it to and fro, for there is no night when you flash this light.

Darkness went and hid when God touched this kid with the arc of his great white flashing. I don't mean to say that it's always full day, and it is for those of us who ask him. For God in all his might, takes a great delight and gives just for the asking.

So let me say to you my friend. I would bow to the Lord and pledge your sword and he'll give you a flash just for the asking.

As I said before, I'm just a fisherman at the door looking for a river to bask in. For fish I adore, but I'll knock on your door looking for more darkness to shine my flash in.

Let me say again my friend pick up your sword and follow the Lord; you can swim with fish if you truly wish and get on your knees and ask him.

For he's a light in the night, and he takes a great delight to flash his light on those who just ask him, and his light is always bright in the very darkest of night; his light never goes dim, so open the door, I'll tell you lots more of this Lord who gives for the asking—so just come to the Lord, pledge your sword, get a touch of his flash, and watch how bright you can make the night. So smile or grin and give a flash again, it's really fun to put darkness on the run. Not because you have to. Just because you ask to!

Nothing looks as good as a flash in the night of a great bright, white light.

The morning star, just come as you are. I Am is coming with his great big flash.

LIFE ON THE GOLDEN STRAND AS I SEE IT FROM WHERE I STAND

When I was small the most important thing in my life was being tall.

When I was young then it was being old enough.

When I was single, the thought was married bliss; before too long, it was enough of this. I'm out of here, stopped for a beer and a little cheer found out all they sold was beer. But what the heck, I hoisted a few. Years went by, a few beers too and one day I "awoke!" To the amazement of quite a few and Lord behold, I was sitting on a pew. The Lord said to me in a voice that I knew, "You're part of my church sit here it really won't hurt you."

So here I am. Life in the new, like a rough-cut diamond, part white, part "light," and a little blue!

To my amusement sitting on this pew! Life's a real wonder—but that's a big book way up yonder saved for his chosen few.

Never knew just when I thought of telling you. Just came to mind in this world I'm passing through.

I don't mind the things I've gone through, now I have a friend that says he's went that way too.

He's kind of like a brother that's always there for you, so time will tell, I guess, if I passed the test, but my brother said I could take a rest, said you worked hard, son, but that's the adventure of life for some now enter into my rest.

Strange, I've been most everywhere some time here, some time there, can't even say where I haven't been, but life sure has changed for me since I met my friend. He was always there; I just didn't see him, guess I was too busy trying to listen to mere men.

Times they change. Same as the wind! I saw him coming with a great big grin. Glad to see yea, he said like a friend; so here we are me and my brother friend.

Holding on to each other, howling like the wind; walking down that golden path in the middle of a river; heck, might be the middle of a great flood for the happy state I'm in, 'cause if I'm not mistaken, a piece of heaven I've entered in.

One thing I know for sure it's a treasure of life to count your brother a friend and know it's real! Walk with your face to the wind, and let the Lord come in.

To my brothers and sisters,

Amen

It's time to write a little of what I hear. Sometimes you can even feel it, and sometimes it just isn't here. The Lord tells me things to say sometimes if I just turn on my ear. Seems to me I read it in his book somewhere, if those with ears would hear.

He told me to tell you he loved you and that you were not to fear. For he watches over those of us that know how to turn on the ears! So that we can speak to you in sign language so that you can hear too.

So if you can read my sign language that means that you can see. So that means you can see and I can hear. So if you can see and I can hear, that means you're somewhere near here.

Guess that's somewhat like God is. He said he's always near and would never leave us; so if we're all this close, it must mean we can all see and hear, guess that must be what sign language is all about.

God's truth and God's fear!

God is very, very near. Amen.

LOVE LITTLE AND A LOT

Love a little, Love a lot. Here's a story that should be taught. So here's to love little, let's just say it's not.

Wrapped up in its self! Kind of a like one big knot! It's hot in the middle and hard on the top!

So why love a little when we can really love a lot. For love is overflowing, kind of like a flower pot. The seed of love keeps growing in a field or in a pot, so don't love a little when you can love a real lot!

Love is in the growing, the pot is just a pot.

So throw your love up in the air, and let it fall everywhere. And when you're down low with despair, can't seem to find love anywhere, just look out your window, sure enough you'll see your love all grown up—not in your pot, but in your lot.

So learn a lesson of a little and a lot. It's not any fun to be little, stuck in a pot, out in the middle of a great big lot.

LIFE

I have not of this worldly lot, but I'll give you what I've got.

First of all, I give you sand and a little salt. It takes sand to make a man, then a bit of clay. Without the clay, the sand would simply blow away with the wind all across this land.

Then comes, water to mix for the potter and a form that you may stand as a man!

Next I give of mine, a mind to call your own, to search for wisdom so you may understand. To that add a little spice, to give a taste for life. I should mention the stars, sun, and moon. The seasons as they play that you may know from day to day! I must give the *word*, that one day your voice may be heard. The wind and the air, breathe the air. Then learn to bend with the wind.

I give vision that you may see, to be all that you can and should be. One more thing I give to thee, I give this ring I call love. It goes around you, sent from above. I call it a robe, yet it fits like a glove, tight as skin this ring I call love.

I give all of this and more. I add truth of soul, stout of heart, and honor that you may do your part and not be left out.

Then I give you, life to live and be as my Father in heaven gave to me.

You may not believe. Love is the gift. The greatest of all these, for God gave his only son that he could love all of you and me and all that will ever be.

For his son came and said, "I Am the way, come and follow me." You'll know my father if you know me.

God's love gave to you, sent through me.

Proverbs 2

WINDOWS

It's dark and cloudy out, you know. Even if you can't see, because you can hear the rumble of the thunder as it travels through your head. One of those days I should have stayed in bed. Except those thoughts kept jumping around that said, "Get up before you go all the way down."

Hear me now as you don't make a sound. Because the sound is sharp, deep inside the heart, when your mind wakes up and says, "You're going down." So now you're up and out of bed.

Your heart's going ninety, thoughts spinning in your head. One thing that stops a thought is something someone said, "When you feel like looking down try looking up instead." The Lord stands waiting, silent over by the bed, then says, "Look out the window, the one that's there by the bed." So you look around and out the window, a blue sky you can see, the sun is shining brightly. It's as nice as it can be. It's a time of life for us that see. We watch the blue sky glowing and enjoy being free. The freedom to call on God, when were lost and going down!

The good Lord, steps right up, and offers his hand. Then I heard him say, "I've never met a stranger, once, I've shook their hand. So remember when in trouble, just cry out, the Lord is by your side. He will shine the light when you think there's no way out. Then this window you will see, for he said to you when he made you know, "This window is here for them that hear when I tell them to see."

So look out, or in the window, hear what you see. For it's that time, so little time, he gives a window from which to see, and says, "I Am the way, the only way, another you will not see."

So look out the window into the sky and follow the Lord. Be alive and free, drink of his cup and don't give up. For he's waiting for the lost! Remember my friend, you can't see out or in the window when you're looking at the ground.

That's what he said to me, "You're not lost, you're found. Now come and follow me."

"Windows we can see," said he to me.

One Way

A man's calling awakes with the son. Some early, some too late and some to be, can hardly wait. Walk with Jesus. It's not too late. Others say, "This is the way to go, today." Follow Paul. He will tell us all. Others say, "Let us follow Peter, he'll teach us to pray." Yet others will say no, "This is the way." We as humans, mere mortal men, try so hard to make God's straight way. Twist or bend, not even knowing the trouble it will get us in!

The baptism of water lets the floodgates down, that the water of life may come in. The streams go the river flow. Lakes hold the water until God says, "Let it go or let it go slow."

If you read the word with the eye of a bird high in the sky, you will see the maker and his how and whys. For the reading of his word is not for all to see, in faith you proceed to understand and learn the ways of your Father's needs. Wisdom he has in his hand, as well as the eagle's eye.

Remember, God chooses the time when you can really see what he wants you to see. So guard your word and hold it close to your breast, for it's a treasure you carry in that chest, the ark of a covenant of things yet to be—God's great plan from before the likes of you and me that sent his son to die in the dark noonday sun. Yet three days away with the breeze would play, as on the way to the Father, went the son that third day, not in a hurry. He stopped and seen some friends so they could wish him well as he went on his way. That day, to Thomas, he had this to say, "Put your hand into my side that you will know it is really I, alive and well as you can feel, as well as see." He was named doubting Thomas ever since.

This message of repentance he gives to his disciples. There's forgiveness of sins for all who turn to me. You are all witnesses of all these things you have heard and seen. Now I'll send the Holy Spirit as my Father promised. When the spirit comes, it will fill you with power from heaven. Power and love from the Father, sent through the Holy Spirit from his son the king of kings, lord of lords. Open the ark, see what you can see.

The one who claims, I Am he, said he to me.

RED SKIES

Red skies in the morning, sailors take warning, so I've heard it said. Then red sky at night is a sailor's delight, around the time for bed.

Jesus walked along the Sea of Galilee seeing a couple of fishermen. Brothers them, Andrew and Simon, called Peter. Jesus called out to them as they were casting their net into the sea and said, "Come and follow me. I will make you fishers of men."

Now it's strange but true. People of the sea are different from most of you. For most are a morality lot in the fact they have been to hell and then back again.

I remember that day way back then and went and followed along with them as they left their lot and went and followed him.

They walked along the shore by the Sea of Galilee when Jesus saw two more sailors that he called out as well to make fishers of men. Their names, James and John to be, so they left all they had with their father and followed after this son of man, that had this plan to free all men, the likes of you and me. They went from town to town around Galilee. Working for God as they followed their Lord Jesus in his teaching of the Scripture, saying repent, the kingdom of heaven is at hand (Mark 1:14).

My friend, that was the start of Jesus preaching the gospel! He grew in stature and fame. Then seeing the many people following, he went to a mount and taught to them what is known as the beatitudes. Blessed are they that believe in the son of God, and doing the works of his Father. He gave himself on the cross. That day, all that believed in him would be saved to salvation and eternal life in the kingdom of heaven. Be blessed of the love of God, our father.

Strange you may say that the first four of his disciples were sailors of the day that he called to catch a multitude of men in their nets.

Then there's a whale of a tale, but that's for Jonah to tell.

What if the Bible had never been written? What if Jesus had never set sail? What if of God, we had never been forgiven? What if no red skies with the setting of the sun, no sailor's delight would you have tonight?

BEAUTIFUL FEET

The reed out in the wilderness! To fulfill John the Baptist's role in the Holy Land, almost eight hundred years before the arrival of Jesus Christ, the messiah. The prophet Isaiah wrote of Jesus coming and his work on earth to be proclaimed the good news (Matt. 3:1-3, Isaiah 40:3).

Those who would receive him would, indeed, be blessed. But those who would share his good news with others would be blessed even more. Lasting happiness is the fruit of accepting Jesus, the source of all good things we are and have, and of sharing the good news and joy with others; when we do this, we become beautiful people and blessed of the Lord. He spoke of family, the value of blood, the saving of Noah and his family and also of Lot, as well as his family, and many others, and as well as the closeness with God, the Father, and also, respect for your own fathers and mothers. Respect for from where you came from, as well as the ones who bore you, the spirit of your family tree (Exod. 20:12). From where you come and all that you will ever be. Your sons and their sons, the linage of life and your heavenly Father who created all that will ever be. Hence, the statement of Jesus, I Am in the Father and the Father is in me. Be true that your children may be proud of where they came and dare to reach to the stars and be assured that God is there.

Jesus said, "I Am the bright morning star." Each of us that enters the realm of heaven and touches the sight of the kingdom and embraces their heavenly Father and comes away with only his love is truly blessed of the kingdom, and all honor and glory will be lavished upon them that finish the race. Make sure your father and mother come in first place with honor and glory. Be thankful. God gave you the grace. Go boldly, give believers strength and guidance according to the anointing of the Holy Spirit for people with beautiful feet (Isa. 52:7).

I Am said to say, "Have you noticed your feet of late." Don't be late; the Lord just can't wait . . .

Butterfly

It flies, it's extraordinary in its beauty and majestic of grand color as it flutters through the air. It's flight of life after a time of death.

Beauty in death, that's the God-given beauty and wonder of the butterfly as it passes by. For it flies to God's clock, not timed as the likes of you and I, a multitude of color and designs, the likes we never knew. Patterns that speak of God and things we never ever knew of. Stopped to ponder in this life we're passing through. Remember, a caterpillar lays down its life that a butterfly may start life anew. I guess that would make the butterfly kind of like I was in my life here that I'm passing on, coming from the dead to walking life in the new with the spirit of the Lord. The caterpillar as well as the butterfly, one and the same, one walked at a crawl and the other flew over the walls. Kind of like, mortal man set up for a fall only to rise again.

The spirit of the Lord makes the fall, a waterfall. Hard to stand under a waterfall and not get wet. Did you ever stop to think, the Lord says, "Those that are thirsty, let them come and drink of my life-giving waters, while you're standing in the waterfall, you're not thirsty once you've drank of my cup."

Just be reminded of the butterfly as we walk through this life with Christ, walk with the grace of God. Travel as a butterfly, pure and true. And people will say, "That man walks with wings, such beauty, such grace, he almost flies standing in place."

THE JUDGE

My time with you, most of you are short in a span of time. It goes as far as the ink of the pen to the end of the paper. Yet enough time to tell you some things from our Lord that he wants me to try to get to you.

It's quite amazing the things we can do today. The simple stroke of a pen can spread all across the country, even to the end of the lands. So let me say here and now, I may not know you and not know where you've been, but I can say if you read this page and get its message that it spreads across this land. Then we can say you are part of God's plan.

The message is clear that he wants you to hear. Remember he is the creator of the universe. Yet he holds you very dear. He said to say right from the start, "No matter what you do, like a child in trouble, he will always be near and will always love you and hold his promise true. If you call to him, he will always answer you."

He said to say and for you to believe, "He's alive, today in everything we do." Sometimes it's a hard lesson to learn. To make sure later we are not the ones that burn, that's a lesson of life, and what he's trying to say to you, through the pen in my hand, is a wake up, to be all that he wants you to be. If you know your Lord and know his Father, God, then do the best that you can for that neighbor of yours and mine. Not once a week or a moment in a day, but in everything you say and do, each and every day.

Hear what he has to say, ask him. He will talk back to you and guide you and see you do all he wants you to. So love your neighbor as he loves you. For if you didn't realize your neighbor is also your loving God. Remember, he said, "Forgive them Father, for they know not what they do." As he gave his life that he could give his love to all of you.

Love your neighbor in all you do that covers all the commands that he gave to you. It's the only thing he demands from you. Have your neighbor do the same as you do. This is the message, remember to pray so you can see, hear, know, and do.

That's the whole of the message he said to give to you and not to fear, as he's right there watching them as they are watching you.

He's the judge in all we do. That's the whole message he gave to me, to give to you. Then to close, he said to say, I Am he, the life and the way.

THE EYES OF GOD

Just the thought of God, scares some folks, and if they even thought that he might see them in all that they do, some would feel shame. I'm sure some would feel pain and can you get a hold of someone so bold, as to say, "What are you looking at?" They'd ask of him.

I can't say for sure but I've heard it said, "Some folks have really died just because they ask him a lie to hide."

I do know of Lot, a Godly man of his lot, the Lord said to go and not look back, but Lot's wife said "what the heck" and looked and died before she could ask him just what he said.

The Lord watches us all, big, tall, thin, and small. He watches with eyes in the sky and rains on us all. It's good to praise him when you call on his name. He likes to be a part of all that we do. If you do for him, he's glad to do for you. And remember, as we pray at night, he has no place to lay his head. He always hears our prayers and sees our hearts to his delight. So stop and think, he's at your beckon call. Live in his will and he always answers your call.

My eyes are everywhere, watching the good and the evil (Prov. 15:3).

Our Lord is alive, looking at the world, using our "eyes" for those of us that have eyes to really see what he wants us to see. Do you hear what he wants you to see? True faith raises the banner of truth for all to see when he's looking at you. He's also looking at me, and it's quite amazing the truth he can see just looking at people just like you and me. By his grace we get to see.

THUNDER AND FLASH

Tomorrow's thunder will be much like the wind that blows across the land or a shooting star as it flashes across the night skies. To let you know there is light in the night. For against the flash of light, not one stood for darkness, for each man that has his cross to bear, also has a mighty sword of light to flash, if he sees a warrior of darkness standing near. Do they dare, with light flashing near, I think not? For with the flash of light the Lord looks from the light and says, "Where or who is there to fear, I see him not standing here."

Tomorrow's thunder maybe here today or may have rolled on by with the clouds up in the sky. But when you see the night flash and hear the terrible crash, you'll know the Lord is near and those who fear will know "whom to fear."

The name is thunder know that it is of God, signs of might; for some, "a delight." As wishing on that first star you see at night, a wonder, nonetheless. Put my thunder to your test and slap my thunder to your chest. Feel the charge, see the light. Did you pass the test of lighting and thunder? Tonight did you praise God as he showed you a great show of his power and might, stronger than we can imagine with our minds and sight, yet knowing of the atom and knowing of the bomb. Should I go on?

Remember my thunder, sing my song, raise your cross, and as a bird of freedom, come fly along. Did I say, "I love my song, thunder, with the Lord, my God! What a lightning rod, what a flash!"

Come to the Lord that he may light your thunder and give you a sword of flash.

His Mighty Arm

A call to arms, a call to arms, that's what he keeps telling me. What does he want to tell us? What does he want us to see?

If we looked, we'd see our kids die in our schools, our children on our streets. What are we supposed to see? What would we hear if he was talking to you and me? Love is from above; the rest is lust and greed of mortal man that we don't really want to see.

A summer night, I see the flash of light ever so bright. Its lights the whole night, the rolling thunder snaps and makes you wonder. Then I hear him say, "The show is of me, all that will ever be is of me. I gave your forefathers this great land and helped them make it free. But somewhere along the way, you turned your backs on my Father and me. So we let you go, to dig your hole and see what a shame you could be."

It reminds me of once I did see, at the Constitutional Convention, Benjamin Franklin was asked, "What have you wrought?" He looked across the land for a while. Then said, with a smile: "A republic, if you can keep it!"

As our God said. "In the beginning was the word" (John 1:1). And the word was made flesh in our Lord Christ Jesus (John 1:14).

Our beginning in this great land he gave to you and me. We started with "we the people."

The sacred rights of mankind are not to be rummaged for, among old parchments or musty records. They are written as with a sun beam in the whole volume of human nature. By the hand of divinity itself and can never be erased or obscured by mortal power (a quote from Alexander Hamilton, 1775).

The Declaration of Independence was the promise given with this great land. The constitution was the beginning of the fulfillment. "Are we the people" letting this great nation die, forsaking our God and creator, your land and mine?

Truth, hope, faith, and trust are the words he keeps giving to me. My Father places words in the air that I may see them. They are words to share with those that still care. He heals with love. Believe, are his cries for the likes of you and me, for it's life to believe and death to the grieved and those that wander on by.

Let me tell you my friend, a story of where I've been, as I watch form here in the sky.

America, are we to die or repent? Is this God sent to you and me?

I HEARD THE WORD

The word in the beginning was and is God.

The word is a beacon that shines his light across this great land. His eyes are everywhere, watching the evil and the good (Prov. 15:3). We are counted as the raindrops that come and are gone, then come again. The living waters that wash the rock and makes productive the desert sand!

God's word is a light that searches the very hearts and mind of man, everyone, as to be counted as wheat for his barn or as "tare weed" to be thrown into the lake of fire, for those he counts not his own. His judgment is true, every time when he says, "I'll have none of you."

If you hurry, you still have time, but *hurry*, for the Lord has a passion for his Father's place that burns within him, and he will not leave one that is out of place.

The word of God has spread all across this land. His winds of truth beckon to look up and search for God. Pledge your heart and all you own to the God that sits on your throne. For the time is short, in fact the Lord is here. He said for me to say with this pen to tell you, "*I Am* the way."

Again I heard him say, "*I Am* the spirit, the son of God and only I have the key to eternity and only I can show you the way. For *I Am* the Lord of each and every day! The truth is you will all see heaven open and the angels of God, going up and down upon the son of man" (John 1:51).

He also said to say, "I assure you, unless you are born again, you can never see the kingdom of God" (John 3:3). And again I hear him say, "Humans can reproduce only human life, but the Holy Spirit gives new life from heaven."

So don't be surprised at my statement that you must be *born again.*

Just as you can hear the wind but can't tell where it comes from or where it is going. So you can't explain how people are born of the spirit (John 3:3-8).

"Truly, *I Am* the way," this is what I heard him say today.

Heartland

It can't be done from the outside. Can it be happening today from within? America, bare your heart. Are we all doing our part to defend this great country that we live in? Or are we letting down our guard because we can't see the darkness that has come in quietly in the thick of night.

We lost prayer in school where God-fearing children learn. We lost the gold standard which tore up the fabric of home. Sent the parents both to work and cut down the family tree. The children won't stay home alone. Then up springs the devil, full of lust and greed. Soon we have our children die in the streets and bleed to death at our feet. We don't see a thing and all ask, "What's wrong."

This country started with "in God we trust." Now he's not even invited in. Our records stuck. We pass the buck and pretend we don't see the end of God's dream.

It's not too late if we stop the hate, tighten our belts, and start to help put back what's right with God. Do good things before we just bust at the seams.

Ask God to rule your house. Forget the "horoscopes" and ask the Lord for faith and hope. Speak the truth, watch for it in all you see and do. If you look and pay attention as you go through your day, it will scare your lights out and ring whistles and bells. People look right through you as if we're all dead.

Again I say, "Awake, pick up the sword of the Lord and pledge your life for the fight."

America, get the Lord in your life. The wounds are real, the blood in our very life, only with God do we have a winning team. Anything else is a small bandage on a large wound. We are sick and sore, lame and blind, lost and alone and wonder why!

We forgot the very words we stood for, "the home of the brave," as we wave from the grave.

Awake to arms. Please ask the Lord to come along! United we stand, divided we fall. We all fall without the Lord and his visions and dreams.

RAINBOW

It's time to write again of what he's telling me! It's like magic this pen he gives to me. For all who can read can plainly see this page of writing he's giving to you and me.

I don't mind, for it's for all to see. The ones that read it and hear what they see that he's talking to, writing through me. For it's a special message that only some will know it's for them, given from him, sent through me.

As the rainbow has no end, a time it's here then gone, only to come back again. It's very elusive, the prism and the hue. It's always here, sometimes out of view. A picture of Christ is what he gives to you. For like the Lord and all he does for you in this life you're passing through. He gives joy and a new song. The rainbow is a promise that he gives in the day for his chosen few. It says he loves you and will always be there for you. Never fear the darkness of night, for just call on the Lord, using his name. There is not a thing in this life he won't do for you in the will of his Father, one and the same, not that he doesn't do for you, but that you know he's there.

That's what he says to say. He wants you to know he's there every day, in every way. He likes to be a part of all and everything you do that the rainbows promise. The Christ in all, his splendor, raising a banner across the sky, in his myriad of color, saying he's always here and will always do for you. He said, "Don't worry they will know just who it is that I'm talking to." He said, "He talks to people in lots of different ways." Like a language of sign. He also uses this pen of mine to tell of the time. Strange, I never know what he wants me to say or even who he's talking to, as I write what he says to say. I know one thing that I can say this day, the rainbow is a path to walk, for it leads to the house of God, and his son will lead the way. So this is for the chosen few that the Lord knows whom he's talking to. Is this person you that he's talking to, today? Are you seeking the words of the rainbow and the path along his way?

I Am said, "The rainbow speaks today."

ANSWER THE CALL

Christp is calling, can't you hear him. Can't you see?

The touch of his presence is as a bud on a branch in the spring. He says it lives. He wants us to come home. He wants us to tell all, we see, his time is near. In fact, he's here with you and me. He say's to make the call, go tell what you hear, from sea to shining sea, and make it clear that all may hear and know the thunder is from me. For from my throne I view mine above, the others I don't even see; for they are not of me and cannot come. When I tell mine, it's time to come home, for I care for my own, the others I swear will not enter into my rest. They can give it their best but not pass the test. So they will see the fire down in Hades, where they will twist and squirm and spend eternity.

All is well with those above, for its plain to see our God and his love. For he alone sent his only son to die for the likes of you and me. Just think, for two thousand years of trials and tears, he has shed his love and grace on the likes of you and me.

Strange, how hard it is to see, yet deny the light of his goodness after all this time. Yet he is still with us, you and me, waiting for us to see his love from above and realize that he wants us to be all that we can be. Then know that he is here, giving forgiveness and salvation with grace to the likes of you and me.

His message is loud and clear; children, come home, your Father is waiting, waiting to take you home.

Christ is calling. He wants you to come home. All Scripture is inspired by God. It straightens us out and teaches us to do what is right (2 Tim. 3:16).

Stay true to what is right, God will save us and all who hear his message. Christ is coming, calling for you and me (1 Tim. 4:16).

He knows whom he calls and knows who will stand or fall. Christ is calling, did you take the call?

Bone and Clay

It's time you hear some of what I'd like you to see. Look at the green grass before it dries and blows away.

Water, the blue in the sky! Listen before it turns to gray and passes into yesterday.

Wait for the sound of time as it passes on its way, it doesn't stop or fiddle as it passes the day. The time is here, then gone to find a new dawn and another day. Did you take the time to pray before your time is gone? Are you still looking for that pot of gold, as life passes on leaving the cold? What is happening to us in this time almost gone? Do the drums beat to a new tune as we sing a new song! Or is it the same old song and you just go along.

Take a deep breath and remind yourself, air is what we breathe and if we clog up our engines of life, the strife is soon to set in. So breath deep, the world is not to fear. For our Lord has overcome the world and he tells us we are not of here and we are not alone.

Put your doubts and questions of life up above and watch it start to rain with all of God's love. For when you ask of him, he is quick to respond, and when you are weak, he gives the strength to go and carry on.

One thing about us as mortal men, we can't control just where we stand or tell the time beyond our span. To live and die, we can only ask why? God says with some thought, "Mortal men are made of clay. Bones return that they may again walk another day. For as your maker, I love my clay, the dawn of life goes on to become a new born day today. *I Am* the maker, and I love my clay. Ask for life. I'll show you the way. Love your neighbor as yourself. I love my clay."

Did I say "*I Am* the way today?"

Home Address

Lord Jesus, your disciples, you sent to all the earth, as a low servant and by your grace, what address would you call my place? How will I know where to call home? So as I ask of thee this day. Please Lord Jesus, answer my prayer and plea? Show us the way to a place we can call our home and know that we didn't stray on the way. I ask in Jesus's name.

I am waiting for your word to touch my ear that my mind might hear, through the message you put in my ear.

A great delight spoke into word has not the defense of truth with the coming of the night. The evil that watches the true will rip, tear, and do all they can do to make a dream disappear into thin air.

So a lesson to the true and fair, speak not of treasures, fine, and fair. For when you reach out for them, evil works will have them, and you will get heartaches and despair. So guard your words with truth and honor. Evil lingers and hides out there. *Readers beware.* I'll run both directions, up and down the mountain, playing king of the mountain or lord of the hill.

So remember, truth of the day can be turned into a lie by the darkness of night, so keep up your courage each day to the end. Go forth in the strength of the Lord. Trust in Jesus. Your savior and Lord, and feed on his own blessed word.

God kept his promise that night when Jesus came to earth. The prophet's message still rings clear. Behold that the king of kings will come again to you. Remember he was here. Next time he'll come as king of kings and lord of lords.

Thanks be to God for his indescribable gift, his son, lifted up. He was to die. He called out "it is finished" for you and me. He laid down his spirit that he might give life to the likes of you and me.

Salvation cannot be won but it can be accepted.

Lord Jesus, I ask once again: What is the address of my new home, in God's heavenly kingdom? Do I get a phone that I may call those left alone?

He Cares

Lord, I feel so lost and alone, not knowing the difference of a rock or a stone. Knowing you're with me, yet I feel the chill of losing my way. Still I know you're leading my day.

Sometimes I ponder with wonder where the path will end. Or truth in fact, if it even began. Yet yonder hills I see the dawn and know this day we must go on. The seasons of life sometimes grow still. Listen, the call of a whippoorwill . . .

I trudge on through the seasons of life, knowing the morrows will bring trouble and strife. Yet in the knowledge of love I find the strength to go on, knowing the spirit of truth and honor. I have found a new song, new hope. I smell in the air, a new way for this man of clay. Spirit-driven, I find I must run and try to catch the evening sun. The winds may blow or the breezes play "I have to go." Come what may, I thank my Lord as I kneel and pray, knowing he's with me the rest of my days. But always listen to praise in the voice as I sing his song. Only I seem to know what I call my God.

I know I must wait till I hear you say, "It's time to go, let us be on the way. Follow me closely so you might not stumble and fall by the way. My path is straight. Hurry, before it's too late. My light is life I shed on some, only given if they want to come. So I say this day, my friend, my spirit is with you forever, even to the end. Watch, you will see me as I walk in the air. My Father sent me, because he cares" (John 3:16)

LISTEN, SEE THE WAY

Have you ever stopped and tried to hear the guy that talks through your inner ear, the one that can't stop trying to get you to hear? Or the same guy that can say, "You have eyes." But you can't see till I want you to see. Or you can only see what I want for you to see.

There's only one voice that talks with you, the others are your imagination, trying to confuse you and tell you things they would like for you to do. Robbers, cheats, and thieves are these, out to do you harm.

With practice, you can tell truth is the light of life. The voice that will show you the way and open your gate! The one that's right on time and is never late! If you'll just stop long enough to listen and see what he wants you to hear. For at your very birth, he quietly says, "I Am the way, I'll show my path to you and guide you with my very light along your way."

Listen, wait and watch for what is not truth of my light. For they come from darkness and will try to talk you into the night and will try and kill my light. So guard my light with your life. Hold it high and shine it very bright. For with a bright light, there is no darkness, and the night will run, and some lost out in the night will find their way in the brightness of your day. The ones that were lost along the way, then give of your light and show them the way. The Lord your God, touched you with grace this day, for I have come to shine this light that you also may find his way.

Ask, your sins are forgiven. Knock and you'll have salvation. Seek and you'll find the path to the kingdom of heaven and the right to touch his throne, if you'll only take his hand and follow him home.

The buds are in the branches on this spring like day. Pledge your sword to the Lord and live to fight another day. Remember you are a man of clay. Your life may end this very day. I've been sent to tell you to repent, repent, and live. The great I Am will show you the way with his bright shining light that you may see the path this day. Yes, talk to him as you pray. Truly, it's the only right way.

I truly mean what I say. Today is the day to find your way. For as you read this. He has already said to you, *"I Am the way."*

LOVE CUP

It's hard to tell what's true in this life I'm passing through. Can't tell if it's a dream, real, or just a movie I've seen on the screen? So I guess I'll take it as a dream. For I saw my Lord spreading his grace! So will hold on to what he has set into place. Faith is the place if you look for his grace. Because he looks from above, and pours out of his, "cup of love" on each and everyone that he loves.

Your tears he can see as he looks at you and me, and tell if they're of joy or any reason you may have to cry, and will wipe your tears and calm your fears and will even tell you why. Ask, he will talk to you. Open his book and take a look in the mirror. What do you see when you look in the mirror? I see the Lord looking back at me. So try to live in his light that he will like what he sees when he's looking back at you.

For to have a Lord that always looks with love when he's looking at you and me is the true meaning we learn about in this life we call "love." For that's the very essence and meaning of the God of life. Love, truth, and faith that his chosen people will find his way! Praise the Lord, call on his name. In the will of his Father, he will give you your dream.

I've heard it said, "Come boldly," but I believe that should be humbly so that we don't stumble with pride, while we take a ride on this "merry go round" we have come to know as life. For Jesus said, "My path is straight, I hold the key of the gate. Hurry that you don't linger and find that I have closed the gate."

I am the way today! Watch out for the darkness of night.

I say again, "Come humbly that you may go boldly in this *love*."

I CROSS MY PATH

My pen ran out of ink, I thought I was done. Then I heard him say, "Get another pen for I have more to say." This is what he said, as he spread his word out on the paper mat where I let the paper and ink play. He said, "I did not come to make you believe in me. Nor did I come to have you deceived of me. I come with a touch of honor for you to see." Truth is what I show that you may see, a way of life that few of this world have ever seen. Only then because it was in my father's plans, they all fell short, for God made plans and his wrath was plain to see if you were a mere mortal man."

"So let me explain, I came to convict not to convince the world. I overcame the world, but I came to convict every single man of his mortal sinful ways that can only bring him to death and hell as well; for mortal man loves darkness more so than light. They like the cover of darkness to do evil in the middle of the night. They think I can't see them out in the dark of night. Little do they know that there's no darkness when I flash my light. My sword of truth cuts through the air with a great flash of light, and thunder crashes when I point my sword. With my mighty right arm, I wipe things out of my way. I don't mean to alarm you, but listen to what I say. The choice is yours it's here today."

The Lord I Am says, "I Am the truth, the light, and the path of the way to my Father's house (John 8:12). I hold the keys to the door. As well the keys to the gate, for those who arrive too late." (Rev. 3:7).

Cast the spell that leads to hell. The choice is yours. Follow me, as I Am the truth. I will set you free or stand at the gate to the path of too late, and the "spell of hell."

I Am said, "*I Am* the son, the power, the Father has given to me" (John 5:22).

I have rang the bell for all my people to tell. This feast is on the Father and me, but only if you have been forgiven. Ask of me for I choose whom I please. It's an honor he has given to me. So ask and we'll see (John 5:22).

If you have ears, it's time to see this message! You see this pen is mine, but the message that you see is the ink that my Lord borrowed from me.

The message is clear, I Am is here, and this is the message given to me, this question is clear. Do you see with your ear? Do you see what you should hear?

Eternity

THE ROCK

Have you ever thought about a rock? The people of old did. For the good book is built on a rock, as well as the world that they lived in! The rock is a rolling stone that covers the tombs that covered the dead, the spirit of life what more can be said. Build on solid rock to stay solid and found, not on the sand where you choke or drown.

The rocks of David, five in his pouch, only took one to kill the giant and the Philistines to rout and run away.

That's what Jesus meant when he said, "This stone shall be called a rock." The very foundation of the world is built of this rock. So what does Jesus mean when he said, "All these shall be torn down?" Then his word says, "The cornerstone which the builders rejected will build it all over again in three days." When he met Peter for the first time, Jesus said to Peter, "I shall call you a rock and upon you will build my church."

A statement of fact, he knew Peter had some grit in his sand and that he would always be a man's man. Even when Peter cried out in doubt as the cock crowed, our Lord Jesus had no doubt, for Jesus knew what Peter was about—that he would be an outspoken voice for his church and the good news of the way!

The church built on Jesus's rock foundation is still alive and well in Christianity to this very day. In fact, I heard him say this very day, "I Am the way today."

"Was I just talking to Peter that day?"

Dream Light

Out of the dark of gloom, right in the middle of the room! The room was a family restaurant. I recalled I had seen her in the middle of the night, when I first saw the flash of light of my Lord that dark and troubled night.

I stood on the seashore of remembrance and looked back at the importance of my life and realized that I really didn't have any reason that I needed to bother saying. For this I stand this day, I had seen the light that night come out of the dark and wind-tossed sea when I talked to God. My thought now is that God really talked to me. I can look back on that time now and see more clearly what was happening to me. For at that time, it was a muddy picture in the mirror that looked back at me, more like a dream. Yet I knew he, the Lord was talking to me about how I might live and do what he needed of me. he only showed me pieces of the picture "frame" at a time, over a span of time. Mostly his time is like walking through a fog. It makes me think of "falling off a log," for I have learned somewhere along the way that if I really listen, I can see what he was trying to say.

It still quite "amazes me" even to this very day, the careful thoughtful way that he guides and glides us along life's way each and every day, if we'd listen to him as we go along the way.

I seem to want to write of this dream, I had that night that I first seen his light. As I started to say, "In a restaurant I saw her that day, the girl in my dream. Out in the dark and lonely windswept sea! That I found myself in, with no way out!" With God all things are possible (Isa. 26:19).

I meet this girl, the one in my dream. I let her know her face I had seen. The Lord had placed her picture in the middle of my dream. So as time went on, love sang a song. So I married this girl, made her my wife, and praised the Lord; we started a new life, it's good to look back in the mirror of yesterday. From the seat of today that we may look into the future to see what the Lord of our righteousness has to say about the picture of tomorrow, as we walk in his presence and live his life, each and every day.

The Lord had this to say to me today, "Arc my lite, flash, the night. I Am, Lord Jesus. We won. My Father and I are one."

PICTURES

A picture of Christ I'd like to be, each and every time someone looks at me. To say that man walks with God, not just in looks would I be this man, but in all I do as I walk the sand. Giving water where there is no well and feeding believers and meeting their needs. That's the picture I'd like to be, if only you could really see me. I'd take each day with a grain of salt, so as to remember what it's all about.

A simple man I'd be. Quite and mild-mannered, if people could just see! I'd pick my words out of the air, because my father puts them there. I'd speak with honor when I spoke to you, because truth and honor go hand in hand, like a handshake, all across the land.

I'd smell the flowers as I went along, most likely I'd hum a song. Course I'm just dreaming as the ink flows or as I can hear Jesus singing the same song. Yes, he is with us as we go along, no matter where or in what we do. I was just thinking to myself, "I sure like that song."

Really a picture is like a song and in all you see and do, Jesus will do.

So here's a picture of a very old song, a picture of Christ in times gone wrong. Of an old rugged cross they made him drag, so I've been told. Yes, he had to carry that cross on his back that black day. The sky went dark, so some say.

I'll not forget that dreadful day and remember the soldiers and what they had to day, "So you're a king." That's what they said to you, as they flogged you in shame. I couldn't hide as all the people came to watch them crucify the Jew, they call king.

I remember well, you see the picture I'm telling you. I Am the man, was and is my king, forever (*eternity*). That's the theme of this team, hard Christian love, that's the picture I saw. He said, "It is finished." That's what he said. We wondered what he meant (John 19:30).

REMEMBRANCE

I speak not to be profound, simply that love maybe found.

Give of your heart to your fellow man, for loving your neighbor works in God's plan. He did not send his son to die in vain or just to say I'll come again. Lord Jesus died for you and me. We hung him in "mayhem" on a couple of trees. The rulers wanted him alive and to set him free, but the people "*we*" wanted his blood not his love.

Stop and think upon that day, it's very much like the one today. Yet it comes down to one last stand. Jesus said, "Forgive them Father, for they know not what they do. But for the love of them, I surrender to you."

It is in giving we seek our Lord, and it is in love we pick up his sword again and again.

Love your neighbor. Make him your friend. Say hi on your way. Or hello as you go. Look around you, make a friend today. Have faith in Jesus, he'll show you the way and comfort your soul. *Yes, this very day.*

Our Lord Jesus died for us that day; but that was yesterday, what about today?

Victory is coming. I can smell him in the air. Yes, he died for us in the days gone past, to make it very clear. Each and every one of us has a cross to bear. For each of us has his death to share.

It's the time to be bold and remember that very day, for it's a time well spent if you repent and call on your Lord today in prayer.

For today, if you repent and ask the Lord to come your way, you'll hear him rejoice and resound today, you have been found.

It is in loving not in being loved. It's a blessing to your heart if you do your part to share the Father's love. Whatever be your longing or your need, for there's no loss when you pick up your cross and follow Jesus. For he said, "*I Am life eternal.* I've been there, my light of love will show you the way, and you will live and love again, TODAY."

The choice is love and life. There's no other way. Jesus won. That's what he said to me, as he hung on that cross made out of a couple of trees.

AMEN

BENEATH HIS FEET

In your mind, you know where to find me. In the kingdom of God, there are lots of doors. Knock on the door no matter where or who you are. I will answer the door. I have the keys. *I am* behind every door in the kingdom of my Father. "*I am* the gate that opens for my sheep. *I am* the shepherd that keeps the evil away" (John 10:7).

In your mind and in your heart you will know and find me on your day when you have a need to bleed from your heart. Ask, I will be there, seek and you will find me. Ask and I will enlighten and refresh you. Call on me and I will call on you. Come and follow me and I will set you free that you may know of my Father that lives in me and I in he.

This world is a crime; do you have the time to endure the pain? Or is it time to lie on the cross and know the love of my Father, my God. Forgive them Father, I made the call. Bless the ones you gave to me, for I give them back to you as I set them free. For I love them as much as you love me. Only mine can hear and see how much I care, for where you are and the what, of all you are. Only mine can see the love you have for them, through me.

The times near for all to see! What they see is what they will be. For judgment on those will come that have never called on me. So forgive them Father, the ones you have given to me that they may help all the rest to see you through me. They do not see that go down and twist as a worm in the lake of fire, yet never burn, sent to be in torment for the rest of eternity.

The time is near. Father help, my chosen in the harvest of flesh that they may see the love shine in the grapes beneath their feet.

In the eye of the mind are the secrets to be found of the love and grace of God from above. That they may find the mountain that was once called the hill of the skull at Calvary that they may see the death of Christ Jesus. That they may find life as you meant it to be.

Glory to the son! For my Father said, "*I Am.*" That's what he said to me. "*I Am* he," he said to me.

THE DAWNING

The dawning of a new day, the early morning light, blue and gray, the birds thrill in the glory of the morning song. The yap of the hounds as they hear you start to move around! The spirit of new birth is the morning sound, a new beginning, a whole new day that until now has yet to be found.

The babbling of the brook, you never hear except at the start of the day. You can almost hear the good Lord say, "I made the world just for you today." So you slow a bit, like the horse takes to the bit and think to yourself, Lord how can I be of help today. For you and this day that I can help to sing the song with you as this day we travel along, knowing that never again will this day, ever be found again.

Stop and think, never in your lifetime will you ever, and I mean ever, will you witness the creation, the glory, the total profound concept of the birth of today and the beginning, the dawning of a whole new world, the start of a complete new day. The awesome thought of a new birth, new life, and yes, new grace of your Lord as yet to be found! Or the start of this wonderful new realization that *I Am* said, "I thought, therefore *I Am. I Am* he of whom he said *I Am*. Life, the start, the beginning, the finish, the end to come around to begin again! *I Am* the master and servant to all that give the call. Ask, it will be given, knock the door will open, seek you will find. These promises I give to those who seek my face and would abide in my heavenly Place."

Watch as holy righteousness takes his place on the throne of the great unknown. Watch as he opens the gate to those he calls his own. I Am the Lord of the day, my friend. Please enter in this day. That's what he said to say. So all I can add is "have a nice day today."

PRAISE DAYS

Time to give thanks for God's favor and glory, and of course, his glory.

We have been chosen, one by one to be his chosen people, each honored in his own time and place, to do the will of the Father and the son of holy righteousness. Our Lord and savior for whom we chose to ask him of his grace, when we found the door to knock at his place.

Nothing in all creation will ever separate us from the love of God once we ask, except and take our place (Rom. 8:39).

God tells the gentiles in the prophecy of Hosea. They were not my people. Now I will call them my people and I will love those I did not love before. Now you are the children of the living God (Rom. 3:29).

Brothers and sisters, we know that God causes everything to work in accordance with his will, to work together for the good of those who love God and are called according to his purpose for them.

By faith, we come to the Lord when called by his Father to service, by grace of Christ Jesus on the cross, is made right with God and forgiven of our sins that lead to death. He did this so that the requirements of the law would be fully accomplished for us that we may follow the spirit of his son and live for all eternity.

For his Holy Spirit speaks to us as God's children, deep in our hearts. Since we are his children, we will share the treasures of heaven for all that God gives to his son. Christ Jesus is ours as well and even if we don't know how to pray, the Holy Spirit interprets perfectly for the Lord and Father. Your every innermost thought of prayer to him for his honor, praise, and glory.

The free gift of God is eternal life through Christ Jesus our Lord, to overcome, the death of sin. Death, where's your victory now? We are free by the grace of God through his son.

Jesus said, "*I Am* the truth, the light, and the way. Come follow me. I'll show you my way and guide you with my light of truth." This is what I heard him say today. Its love and praise of the son and the Father kind of day! See, the spirit knows, he tells me what to say, as well as when to say it.

THE SPIRIT SPEAKS

Keep your sights high if you expect Jesus to come into view. For our Lord takes his place in your space and loves in your place once you take him by the hand. He's strong and gentle.

I write this note not to impress you but to guide you in the path you chose. We have only the "good news" to guard us in our hearts.

It's God who saved us and chose us to live a holy life. He did this not because we deserved it, but because that was his plan long before the world began. To show his love and kindness to us through Christ Jesus and now has made it clear to us by the coming of our Lord. To each of us, as our savior who broke the power of death. Then showed us the way to everlasting life by the "good news." So stay strong in the strength of the Lord. Remember to love in the faith and love that you have in Christ Jesus, the Holy Spirit which lives within us. Guards what has been entrusted to us.

Teach these truths to others in kindness and humility and the strength of the spirit that they may pass the good news to others.

Follow the Lord, listen to your heart. What did you go out into the wilderness to see, a reed blowing in the wind? Look, I send my messenger before you. Anyone who welcomes you is also welcoming me and the Father who sent me. If you welcome a prophet, you will get the reward of like kind. If you welcome good godly people, you will be given a reward, and if you give even a cup of water to a little one of mine, you will surely be rewarded.

God blesses those who are not offended of me. To experience God's strength, we must recognize our own weaknesses.

Remember that he calls us by name, what privilege to place our faith in Christ. God loves us more than we can even imagine and promised to never let us go. Do you hear him calling you? Christ Jesus knows your need, your name and your face. God has called. He has made mention on my name (Isa. 49:1).

We know that God causes everything to work together for the good of those who love God and are called according to his purpose for them. Because of Christ, we have been adopted into the family of God to share and to suffer (Rom. 8:15). We as Christians, as vessels of the living God walk by the movement of the Holy Spirit. Listen carefully, watch. Again, I say watch.

I Am here, today.

ASK

How do we live without the Lord and God in our lives? Thinking we're smooth. Living life on the edge, not even knowing all the time, we're dying or dead, never knowing just what lies ahead, wandering around in the darkness. We sometimes like the night and would just as soon spend the days lounging in bed, or out spreading our lust and greed to all in the world that might gave a need. Crime and corruption are a job of man's works of spreading the seeds of weeds.

"Ask." Enter the Lord in the middle of the night with the touch of his sword, came a great flash of light. "Why are you trying to kill me?" I heard him say. I said, "What have I ever done to you? Just who are you and what's all this light? It's the middle of the night." Then I heard him say, "This night, I strike your darkness and turn your night into light. Your works of darkness and man's work will die with you tonight. I have chosen you to guide and guard my light. My sword is the light of truth. So with my grace, I wipe clean all I hold against you. From this day forth, you have my light, a sword of great might, to strike at the darkness and turn the night into light."

Did I think to say that each and every day I take the time to praise and pray to my Lord, as I proudly go to work, in the work of the Lord? I carry ink in my mighty Lord's sword and try to strike whenever he gives me a hand. For I make no claim of the words that come out of the pen I find in my hand.

He told me to say to all the people as I went along my way that the word of the day is *"ask."* He will tell you what to say if you don't think you know the proper way. So you're down and out, lost and alone, call on the Lord and look for his word, the pen in my hand as the light of his sword.

I hear him say, "Truly, *I Am* the life and the way. Call on me if you've lost your way. Ask. Follow me. I'll show you my way with a new day today."

That's what he said to say. So have a nice day today. *Ask.*

SIMPLE TRUTH

Simple words as I think of you, I say simply because they are true. A lie may work for a short time, but the truth will work for all times through and through. I don't mean in the things you say and do, for they may be true to you.

I speak of God and his words so true. Speak his truth. Honor will follow you. Grace from you will not hide, for with truth does grace abide.

Kindness is a language that's easy to see and hard to hide. It's a voice that the deaf can hear and the blind can feel. So all can see kindness in you and me!

Remember truth in all you do. What you say today may be used against you tomorrow, make sure it was the truth.

Silence, is better that the truth sent in the wrong direction. Truth, like a half-truth sent in the wrong direction end up as a lie (by intent).

Up and down, Christ and the truth are alike in this respect, one and the same. Hades and hell, one and the same! The maker of lies is the deceiver of the truth, as well as the deceiver of the truth, it's the maker of lies.

Truth and life are drunk from the same cup; make sure it's God's cup you use.

Freedom rings free, as long as truth rings free. It was said, "Give me liberty or give me death." Christ Jesus said, "Give them life that I may overcome their death." Your path in life is measured by your truth.

Christ Jesus said, "I Am the bright morning star."
Thoughts on truth light, lies and darkness of night.

1. In the light of thirty silver coins, one truth walked away, darkness got none.
2. In the light of truth, there is no darkness, not even one.
3. The best way to show off lies is to turn on the light.
4. One thought on life (truth)

Truth, life eternal for those who dance with me! I Am the gift and the prize; those who can hear open your eyes.

These are just simple truths that I hold very dear. Truth, honor, and valor are always easy to see, when in Christ Jesus we believe.

This is the simple truth as he told it to me. He said, "*I Am* he of whom he said *I Am*. *I Am* the truth, life, and the way."

WHEN JUSTICE PREVAILS

When justice prevails, the Lord your God will set and trim your sails. He'll set your course and master the helm and never a fear will you see, no shipwrecks or disasters at sea, only smooth sailing for you and me.

Truth and honor will free. Honesty will live in every home you see. Children will have fun and laughter in all they do and see.

I speak not of the justice we've got, for it's hard to see. Do you see any killers and reapers soon go free, even as they build more prisons for the likes of you and me. For corruption and greed have planted the seed in most all you see!

Our children today have this to say, "Why is everybody wearing the hood and trying to shoot back at me." Yet we still don't see, because we didn't believe when God sent his son. We yelled, "Crucify, crucify." Not hearing our Lord that day, not hearing him say, "Forgive them Father. They know not what they do."

Strange as it seems, I see in my dreams the works of man die, according to God's plan. We will all hear God say, "I declare this day my son will have his way. He will take back this land and judge each and every man to either his rest or, to the pits of hell to join the rest that fell."

All of us that wanted our own way, will you change your mind? Will the Lord you find? Admit you're wrong and change your ways. Are you listening? Can you hear him say, "*I Am the way, the truth, and the light!*" I have come today, this day to expose the darkness that lingers in the night and tries to stay out of sight. For they can't last in the light of the Lord's flash, when he strikes his sword with his mighty crash." I heard him say in my dreams tell the people what you've seem (Luke 7:31-35).

I care not if you listen or not, for he told me he knows the people of his lot, not the sheep of the flock. If you know of him, he's here. If you don't know of him, you simply see thin air. He's only here for you, if you know he's true. If you care, he cares for you and your name is in the Book of Life. He already knows your name.

John called out in the desert two thousand years ago to proclaim the coming of the king. I'm telling you again the same thing. Now he's the king of kings, and my name's not John. But I know for sure when he recorded my name, he just changed the name in the psalm (Matt. 11:10).

GRACE********
AMAZING AMUSE

Grace is really as much amusing as it is amazing in the sense that first comes the word, the way and the life, and I guess that I should say on the way a little light, or is it a little light, that comes from bright to dim, and all the way in between, that's for the ones that's not quite bright can still see him as I was about to say, he's really a lot of fun once you know how to see him, he's lean and mean to those that don't know him, but once you ask, it's a blast, it don't take long to get to know him, ever hear, I laughed till I cried, well I laughed till I fell off my cloud, and have nothing to hide except a little pride when I shouted out loud when I fell on the crowd . . .

Jesus just grinned as he picked me up again, well I scraped my hide, as well as my pride, but I'm ready to go again, it's really who you know if you really want to grin.

When Jesus said joy to the world, I didn't understand what he was talking about? Himself, I thought he meant to grin.

I'm amazed at the word (amuse), because then you have another one, amusing, and another, amused, what a find, as I pass the time, playing with my Lord, it's hard to get bored playing with the Lord and knowing he calls you friend . . .

I haven't said much, just mused somewhat about amuse, it's just the back side of abuse or abused or abusing, I guess that's the other side of light, that's where my Lord, Jesus, would like to stick his (sword), course we'll just call it his (light) tonight . . .

He is a wonder, Lord Jesus

PIRATE AND THE SAND

I was a crusty old pirate once, flying the stormy seas. All primed for life in all the nasty ways like in those olden days.

Surely, just as nasty and drunk and just as dumb with rum as the one's of old and most assuredly just as bold.

I heard myself say just as plain as the day. I'm the captain of this ship to any a man I'll make my claim. I'll put his back to the rack and chains. It's my time, I want every dime and all the things that are fine.

Like the pictures of old, taken of the bold, mostly the clothes is what you see, because the clothes make the men. The man makes the stand and sticks in his claw the most that he can.

God gave not of this lot and said this day, "I'm going to take all that you've got, as I think you're a wretch of a man."

I'll take a whip to your side and rip your hide if you don't listen to me.

Get on your feet before you get beat. I'll make you a man if anyone can.

God said, you'll stand by my side and do what I bid, or with the ship's anchor, you'll lay on my bed with the rest of the dead lying on the bottom of the sea.

Let it be said, I'll do as you said, I'm already dead. Lying at the bottom of the sea!

But I see a life free from strife with this one you've given to me. So I stood by his side, my eyes opened wide, I nearly cried. For this treasure he was giving to me, she was a real beauty as anyone could see.

So did I forget to say, I died for him that day.

Needless to say, mate, he had his way, he gave me a new life, free of strife, worry, and greed, even a treasure he gave to me.

Did I forget to say? He just raised his hand, and the ship sailed away with the rest of the pirate band.

So today, I'm home, lads, one thing more to say—it's good to have my feet in the sand. Just one of the guys listening to the band!

Honey, wake up, open your eyes, you've been asleep since three!

EVERY DAY NEEDS

Sometimes when you're feeling blue, nothing right in your life and you don't know what to do. I would like to take the time and offer my hand to you. For if your burden is heavy, he'll lighten your load for you! I must say and this is very true, I also see some humor in what I offer you, but believe. Ask the Lord of my life, and if he's busy, you might ask my wife; for like me, she's in love with God for life.

My Lord is love or truth and faith of another name, the God of all creation and all we can't explain but make no mistake. He knows just how to play what we know as life's little game.

He's here in the morning, with a smile on his face and asks if we'd like some breakfast, maybe a little grace. He's with me through the day; when I'm on the run, he makes me take the time to pray and at times I can kind of hear him say, keep it up, this is kind of fun.

And of course, he's with us, at the close of the day, as I sit down in my chair. I can sometimes hear him say, this has been a fun day, and as we get ready for bed, let it be said, as we close the day, he is there as we pray and very serious, where he points to his heavenly Father, and says I Am the way.

Yes, my friend, you can call on my God, my Lord, can also make your day, he'll even teach you to pray, my Lord got every day for those of us who pray.

It's helping a neighbor as he goes along life's way or building a bridge to cross, or building a home so he can put in a bed, or just a place to spend the night as a friend.

Loving is not just saying something nice; it's also doing, sometimes at great personal price. One thing about walking with the Lord, he's there to help us as we meet his needs and one thing about it, it's hard to get bored when you walk with my Lord.

So as I was saying, yes I'm talking to you. If you find yourself in a time of great trial and need, give a call to Jesus. My Lord will meet your needs.

KNIGHTED WITH LIGHT

It was one of those nights for me, I was praying to my Lord on my knees in prayer.

I handed the Lord my sword, and as he took it in his hands, it began to glow, and as he admired it, it began to grow, and he said this is one of my finest, and gave it back to me.

Then he said to me, my son, this night, this very night, I knight you with my light, where truth will shine as bright as my light, so take this day and take this night and with the power of your heavenly Father, shine your light bright into the night.

My Lord told John, the lame walk, the blind see, the poor are fed, and the sick are healed . . . Then he said, go forth and tell the people of the things yet to be.

For this night, this very night, your Father and God has this night lighted thee with his light that I may go forth and shine his truth into the night and make it very, very bright . . .

I can hardly believe with all his power and might. That he would give this kid this great big light to poke in the night. Make no mistake, my Lord, my God, lit this LIGHT . . .

NOW LOOK AT MY SWORD!

HONEY BEE TREE

My light flashes across the paper and writes a message of claim for all to see, for a thought of remembrance my mind has made to be.

The storms roll in on a sailor, and squalls you can plainly see, but it's always nice when fair weather returns, to know the good Lord watches over thee . . .

POTS OF GOLD, are good for the soul, and a rainbow brings remembrance of times gone past, for the times of old, was a time of the bold, valor, honor, and glory are things you could often have, the grace of God to thee.

Those things have been, I look back and kind of grin, see those treasures were mine, once upon a time, for as a young sailor, I also played in the sea.

A captain this kid, out looking for treasures that were hid, I looked high and low, wondering which way to go, before I heard the Lord say to me, the treasures I hid in the deep stay hid, I forbid . . . leave them to the bottom of the sea, come with me, my friend, I'll make you a fisher of men; it took some time, I left all behind and followed this Lord of mine.

It's a rocky road out in the sand, the thistles and thorns tend to make you forlorn and have fell by the way, lesser of men, but to the bold that say pray to the Lord, I hold and pledge my heart, this day, it's like a dream . . . honey, milk, and cream.

There's fish in the sea worth a dime every time, but I'll take the Lord's honey for me, so it came down to this, eat fish if you wish, but with the Lord, I never get bored, and that's real life to me . . . !

A garden, free of worry and strife the Lord has given to me, and I might add, I'm happy and glad . . . my Lord just keeps giving to me . . .

The secret it seems is as the light beams, all to God's glory, a wonder . . . I work a garden, most men never even see, but that's my Lord's glory, and me and his honey bee's tree . . .

A SHAME

It's a shame that we can't see him, because it's so hard to believe, yet if we could see him, just what would we believe.

Jesus walked on this earth before. Did all believe that saw him? The answer my friend is no. The whys and wherefores I don't surmise to know!

Believing comes from the heart, it's the faith in God, as we let him do his part, remember he created all the earth and, yes, all the universe too, then he rested for a day, he didn't say now I'll go away. He made promises, so the Scriptures say, and he is still doing them to this very day.

Just by faith alone we should give him our praise and thanks and mean it to the very bone, for when he made us, we were made of clay.

Yes, it's quite a shame we don't try to find his love. Instead, all we do is try to push and shove . . . and ignore the one we should really love.

He'd show us how much he really cares if we'd take the time to see, he even sent his only son to die for you and me, thinking then, we would look up and truly see all the love he really has for the likes of you and me.

But no, we simply say, I can find my own way for I can see as plain as day, as you walk into that tree or wall; so he says suit yourself, please don't hurt my tree or wall as you stumble and fall, beating your head against my wall.

Why don't we understand, he doesn't need to be seen, his eyes are all around, looking for the lost that they may be found, it's not our touch that makes him real, it's how we feel in our hearts that makes him real.

It's how you hear, as you go on your way, when he says, I love you child, what did you hear him say?

Shame of it is, I'm sorry, I have to say, we think of ourselves, too much of ourselves, I'm really sad to say, that we can't really see. Don't hear what he has to say.

We don't feel his presence. We don't call out his name. Yes most of us don't even take the time to pray . . .

It's a shame. Yes, can't you hear Jesus say, I Am the way!

Hear, to see, see to hear, listen, he says it very clear, open your hearts, I Am standing right near, waiting . . .

FORGET ME NOT'S FOR ME

A flash of the past, I can tell you at last, time of remembrance, things I have seen, maybe in a dream, none the less, a true treasure given to me.

My Lord, my God, makes it kind of hard, sometimes he gives of me a delightful crumb, I want to tell someone, yet he tells me, it's not time for them to see, so I flash my light out into the night, hoping someone will come and see, 'cause if they can hear my light out in the night, I'll know it's time for them to see, all that God has chosen to enlighten to me; for what he gives to me costs not a dime, you see, yet is true to the bone, through this fiber of mine, I forget me not, that he gave me this lot that we hoe. And grow and spend our time, it's not much. When you speak of such, one thing is for sure . . .

If you love and know how to grow and work your, hoe! Into the ground! Love will grow, soon you'll have love on your lot, and if you're a farmer, you'll understand, a good crop is worth a lot, so let your love grow out in your lot and people will hear what you want them to see, love, all grown up on your lot and it's free . . . Before too long it grows into trees and flowers with honey bees, and before too long, it's just a nice place to be; so come spend some time take some love on home for planting time, meet my friends, they're here for life . . .

That's my friend, Jesus, over talking to my wife. He's got her growing this love and stuff . . . !

Once he told me about a rainbow in a funny kind of way; he said all kinds of flowers and fruits and things make for all kinds of colors and forget me not's, bring rainbows in splendor with golden pots, a true God-given glory grown right in the middle of your loving; thanks a lot, the love is in the growing, thank the Lord Jesus for this.

FORGET ME NOT . . . AMEN

America

The land of the beautiful, the home of the brave, proud and free, *God's* chosen land he gave to thee and me.

Turn around and try not to cry. Don't bother to ask the where and the why, in the rocket's red glare, the bombs bursting in air, gave proof that our flag was still there!

God said "trust in me, I'll be there with you. Oh, say can you see what you're doing to me. I'm with you in your time of trial and of your every need, yet you look around and don't even see the need, still *I Am* with you. A chosen people I call my own, a great land, for them to call their own. Yet in their darkness, yes, dark skies of grief and trouble, you closed your eyes and never bothered to call on me."

I see you every day and watch over you each night, each day as you go along your way, you push and shove and say "get out of the my way."

Yes, I sit and cry for you, my people, as the years pass on by and wonder if you think to use your ears to hear what you should hear, or feel that I would heal, if you'd just turn to *me*; the old have lost the vision I gave with this great land; the young never knew or thought that they might one day be able to see, nor were they ever taught to get on their knees to pray, or whisper a prayer that they might care, parents simply say go outside and stay out of the way . . .

So beware you people of the darkness of time; for the devils got his hand on this great land of mine. The world's about to see; things start to happen beyond their wildest dreams, watch, wait, and listen. The *Lord* has crossed the fiord to reclaim this land of mine. The flash of God's sword will be raised by the *Lord*. The cut will be true. Yes, what power you will see. The wrath of the *Lord* with his sword and the love from above!

Remember *America, Jesus* said, "I have come to save the world." Will a holy war knock on your door! Did you bother to pray to the *Lord* today? Who said "I Am the *way*" . . . *today*!

FRIEND

I have come to save the world, I hear him say to me; a little at a time, most will not even see, for they have to see life sitting in a tree, if they ever want to get a glimpse of me, my hugs and kisses, I give away free, but so as to not offend, I wait for them to ask of me . . .

I blow my horn as quite a tune for the lost and forlorn, that they may come and follow me.

It gets better once they have been reborn, not to say no more trouble and strife, for they give direction and meaning to life, to learn the meaning of friend and amen.

It's nice to understand that once you ask *Lord Jesus* to be the *Lord* of your life, you have a personal friend the rest of your life. Even if in your mind you have doubt and want to cry out and don't care so much, stand still, you can feel his soft caring touch there to comfort you . . .

When you think you've lost your way, stop and listen, you'll hear him say I'll guide you the rest of the way.

There will never be a day in your life that you'll not have a friend to be a helper through the day or help you to pray or even as to what to say.

Never a worry is what he wants for you, think not of tomorrow for each day he will guide you through; remember the flowers out in the field, he'll ask, did you grow them; and you'll say no, then you'll hear him say did . . .

If you really want a friend as you walk in this world of need and greed, talk and walk with Jesus, your *Lord*; he's got all your needs, and his truth stands in the way of your greed.

Make your way his way, know without a doubt you will walk and talk every day in every way in the kingdom of heaven and will have the gift of life, that's life . . .

You will never have a problem, you cannot overcome, if you take the Lord with you and take the time to pray, he's the one that say's *I Am*—the *way*.

As a friend, seek me, and you will find the kingdom or seek the kingdom of *God* and also find the way to I *Am* . . .

Kingdom of God
I Am,
Friend

HOME OF THE FREE

See the corruption that has spread across this land, all due to the lust and greed of evil forces placed in mortal man's hands.

We forget that when God said love thy neighbor, neighbor is also you and I.

America has forgotten that our Lord and God gave us charge of our course and like a ship lost at sea, we can see the wreckage and the lost that we have come to be.

Our children are left lost and alone, we wonder why, they don't even want to come home. Not being taught of God and love, they do it on their own, to get a share. They only know to push and shove or steal or kill, and they say, "What's the big deal?"

Too often, we are all left alone at home, watching the phone, wanting to talk to someone. We don't stop to think, we can talk to the *Lord* any time we're bored and alone, and afraid, any time for anything and don't even need the phone.

We are not alone. Ask, he'll talk to you. Ask forgiveness. Tell him where you've been. In the blink of your eye, he'll forgive your sins and explain in simple truth and love how you can begin again. For as soon as you say you're sorry and talk to him, your burden gets light, and you have a friend of him day and night for the rest of your life. Yes, a gift of God's eternal life. The only thing you have to do is turn on your light.

Wake up people, stand and do what's right, for this land was given to us by God to shine his truth, to beam his light out into the night, that the world may see the land of the free and the privileged, to love one another, and to be a neighbor, friend, and to be all that we can be, that's what he meant for us to be. For the whole world to see that we stand in the light of his might and do what is right, that's what God meant us to be.

Sons and daughters of God, people standing united, in the land of the free, the land that your God gave to you and me.

Father, forgive them. They just don't seem to hear or see. My friend said this to me (1 Cor. 13:13). Why does God give so much credit to *love*?

Starlight

I Am the bright morning star. I stand in the view, whether close or from afar.

I Am, the alpha and the omega, the beginning and the end. "I Am he, he said to me. Listen closely, my message is clear. The river is worthy and is overflowing near here,

Drink of my cup. Salvation is here. See, I Am coming. In fact, I Am right here. He is over there, and he's always very near.

I Am, both the source of David and heir of the throne.

You see me in the morning if you stop and take the time. I bring the morning light that overtakes the night. I Am the bright morning star, if you see me, you know I Am near and never very far. Stop and listen. Know I Am God. Listen to the silence and hear the inner thunder and know that it is I.

I can light up your life as easy as I light the morning sky. My mission is life, seek my face. Look in my eye; I Am inner peace as well as creator of earth, water, and sky. I Am, the fire that flashes across the darkness of a troubled cloudy sky. "Yes" *I Am* all things, the where and the why. Closer than a thought to every human being! I Am the very reason for every living thing.

I Am, the source, the Lord of your life. I send this message to all those that hear, the Lord is alive. He said to say to this man of clay, spread my word, knock on the door, light this light, and shine out the darkness, make it bright; yes, ask, be a star. Let the cup of the Lord spill into your life.

Oh, he said to say he loves you, be the star that he's seen in your eye. He will be with you each and every day. That's what he said to say.

I AM is the Star of the day and the message is Light.

All who are victorious will inherit all these blessings, I will be their God, and they will be my children (Rev. 21:7).

GREAT DELIGHTS

Words to Hear

A great delight! Spoke in to the air. If not heard is soon not there.

To speak a truth, then tell a lie, shake your head then walk on by; it can't be the truth if backed by a lie. The speaker looks and no one's there. The wages of the lie is total despair. So guard your words, make sure truth lives there. Speak softly, true, and fair, and you'll find an ear standing near. That ear hears that's standing there. Truth is a badge of honor, not many earn or wear; but it's a truth of life to those who have faith and care.

One day, they can say he did his part. He did his share. One moment you look at life, the next it isn't there. Only by the grace of God do we linger here. Life is a moment we all get to share. Live it the best you can. Stand proud to give a hand, a time to care. Love is eternal; if not for love, someone to share and know that you care. The love in your heart and the love of God above! With love and with none to share the song of love would surely die if there was none to care. Life would turn to stone, and the life-giving rock would turn to stone, and the life-giving rock would just be a rock. So let your love song fill the air, and let it be heard of those that care, because a love song needs to be sang to tell those that care to join in the song.

For a great delight needs to be sang, to tune the winds and the reeds that bend, give voice to the word and see who comes along.

Let truth be your great delight as the light shines in your sons and daughters' eyes. Yes, sing a love song and see who comes along, the burden is light and he lights the night and shows the way to those who stray. His path is right. His love is his light and ask of him. He is the way.

Did I hear him say, "I Am, the way." I take great delight in the song of his word and the love that re-sounds with each given word. What song is to be sang this day or what given word to use as we kneel to pray.

Father, I call on the name of your son for my song, Jesus, Jesus, Jesus, there's something about that name when I say it. I see a flame, a candle, a light. Yes, *I Am* says, "I Am the way, the light and the life." Light my candle to light your way, and soon you'll see me. *I Am* the way the light and the life.

I take great delight.

We're on the way, this very day were. Not to blame, we've been chosen, we have no shame and we're not to blame.

We were naked once, for all to see. Now we're clothed in light, and it's really very bright, for the Lord wants us to see in all his glory and honor all his majesty! For us his praise, honor, and glory are for us to share.

We shine his light for some to see, but only the chosen ones can really see. We talk to others and give a word to hear, but one they hear they will also see.

So it's open your ears and see what you hear. He's not over there; he's standing right here. Yes, right with you and me waiting for you to hear what he wants you to see.

If we can open our hearts as wide as we can he'll take a walk with us across the sand.

Not the sand of the desert where others have gone and been but he'll walk with us on the "sands of the golden strand."

That's the golden street of God's great wonderland; it's called his majestic kingdom, and truth honor and justice make up his very throne. He wants us to join him. He doesn't like to live alone.

Hail the Lord

Hail the emperor, hail the king, praise the Lord for what he brings and ask your Father for all good things; yes, ask the creator of the universe and the Creation of all that it means.

Then praise your Father in heaven and give thanks to the Lord. Ask of his word, be given to you, that you may discern the right and truth of things as they begin to burn. For Jesus our Lord and savior, brought truth to the world! That we may have light and the hue of darkness has lost its glow. For when the truth is placed in your mind the darkness is hard to find. It hides in doorways or just out of sight or slinks off with treachery, to do evil out in the night.

So take the sword of the Lord and strike into the night and watch the flame of truth come into sight and let the demons of darkness run for their lives. For once, they see God's armor shinning so bright, they run and hide. For all God's people can make darkness bright and swing the sword of life and light, and they say I am of the Lord's, so who is there to fear.

So let me say again and make myself clear: Hail your emperor, hail your chief, but give your God your whole belief and accept the Lord as you hear him say, "Come follow me, I Am the way." So take your suit of armor, given of the Lord and take the sword of honor with the light of the Lord, then listen to see what you can hear, as your God and Lord says where are they to fear, I'm standing right here looking for a fight tonight. Not a shadow of darkness. Only truth shines this bright. What a night light the early morning star has come.

Stay bright tonight that they may see the way. Yes, I heard him say,

"I am the way."

CRYSTAL BELL

Its dinnertime, the bell has rung.

What do you see in the rays of the sun? Do you see the warmth of it, do you see the glisten of the penetration of the energy of life into your soul, or do you see what it means to all that was, or what it is to all that will ever be?

The Lord shines his light on the evil and the good. He gives his water to drink, for all there is, is his. Like the butterfly in all its beauty and splendor, so beautiful then gone. Did it just fly away? Or did it find a new beginning, a new dawn? Did it start again, or is it just gone? Where is it today?

Do you see the prisms in the crystal, as the light hits the dew in the early dawn! Does the light stop there or does life go on?

Life is a question you have to ask of light; there is no life in darkness I fear. Do you see all of this and still not hear. I'm afraid it's true. For I Am of my Father and I ask of you, that you may tell your sons and daughters, do you own this light that my Father gave to you? That I gave freely to this world. I was just passing through.

Time will tell just who rang the bell. The sound rolls on over yonder and dell. Where it stops, only one can tell. For in the beginning, *I am* came to tell there was only one bell. It rang loud, clear, and true. Yes true, clear, and loud. And its ring today is still there, the dinner bell has rung.

My Lord, Jesus, has come, saying I am the way, my path is light. The banquet is ready, won't you please come? The blind see, the deaf hear, and my message is very, very clear.

I Am is here with his Father. It's time to partake. Come sit down to eat this feast of love, the banquet from above! Did you hear the bell?

I Am, will tell his Father these are mine, I saved from hell!

LISTEN,
KING ONCE,
KING AGAIN

I was a Viking once, way back when, with a Viking sword pledged to my king. Prime for the time and the heat of the battle! I took the line of the sun by day and danced with the stars of night. My vessel was sleek and swift when we'd take what we wanted and sing hail to our king and cross the seas. You could hear our swords ring, plundering the land in the name of our king, doing all the bad, good things. I looked behind myself one day at all the carnage and death of that day, and fell on my knees, as I felt the need to pray, and thought of my Father and wondered just what he'd have to say of his victorious son that fought every battle and prevailed and won. Doing the bad things, not hearing the sounds of the lost and forlorn! For when it was over, I thought we had won, knowing all these bad things I had done.

I found myself in prayer as I awoke from my stare and heard this voice out in the night, and cried out "who is there," and a light of brilliance appeared out of the air. The voice said, "Fear not, I Am is here, I have come to help you see what you don't seem to hear. So listen to my message, open your ear, for when I speak my message is very, very clear. Truth, honor, valor are for the very bold, that they may go forth and spread justice and tell the people, the ones that wouldn't hear, that the day of judgment has begun. The time of sorrows for the ones that don't fear what they should fear, for as I said, I Am the king, I Am the creator of everything. I Am God of all good things. Truth, honor, and love from above, "These I hold true and dear, I fear."

This day, I say to my son, I have seen the things that you've done; the good deeds were few. As you plundered with that band and all the bad things that you did cannot be hid under the shadow of being a son!

So this I say my son, go forth to all the land, tell the people just where you stand. Be a Viking again. With truth and honor make your stand, raise your sword across this land and say, "This day, I pledge this sword to the Lord." A Viking as I stand, a foreigner in a strange land, an ambassador to be from sea to shining sea.

Knighted with light, I'll stand and fight and pledge my sword to the Lord. I came to fight for my King. Surrender to love from above, and *live*!

Jesus Today

The life and times of Jesus our Lord as we know him today! I guess you can say he wears blue jeans; of course, a lot of other things too—like maybe a hippie statement or a farmer too. Makes you wonder just what he drives. Maybe a bus with flowers on the side, to take his brethren with him by his side! Or maybe a Ford, with four on the floor. Saying "Out of my way, I'm the Lord!" It's hard to say just what he's doing today, but his sayings are as true today as they were yesterday.

He doesn't go bragging around, saying "I Am the son." He's quiet and gentle, more so than some, he mentions he knows you even by name, and quite amazed if you call him by name. He likes to talk of truth and will even give proof and once in a while! He'll mention his light. One thing I noticed when he talks of light, he never seems to mention all of his might, he talks of his Father, and he shines so bright, always giving credit to him for what he does with his light. He loves today as if tomorrow might not come. In a way, I guess that will be true for some. For a truth he imparts to some who will claim a life eternal, if we will call on his name. For if we'll open our hearts' door and ask him to join us, we'll live with him forevermore, and once he comes in, then he will open his door and make you so happy, you'll cry out for more.

Life is a journey he wants you to see; that's why he likes the seashore, to walk in the sand, so he can show you the way, his way; life's a dream, so it would seem, and he says it is, if you'll hold on to him . . .

Remember, he's the bright morning *star*. He can do too, for or through, that's where dreams come from (prayer). He always listens. He's always there and always cares. That's *Jesus*, today; so *praise the Lord* today.

Pray that he knows your name today, in *Jesus's* name.

THE LIFE, THE CALL

Into the hands of the rulers of darkness, he was betrayed by one of his own chosen for a mere thirty pieces of silver—to be crucified as a traitor, in front of all the people, that they might not believe on his word that he was not the messiah, the son of God, the king of the Jews, that he was not the Christ Jesus, born in Bethlehem, to shepherd his sheep, the Jews, and the nation of Israel with his Father's guidance, and save the lost. All for the sum of thirty shekels of silver, in the mist of darkness, beaten and shamed, flogged and nailed to a cross, placed between two criminals on the hill of the skull, on the mount of Calvary. Yet true to the truth of his Father in heaven, he was raised the third day and ascended to the throne of *God*, his Father. To defeat all that was not truth and life. Praise our *God* almighty for the gift of his *son*, that gives light to the world, found the lost, gave death to darkness, and all the evil force that by faith in the son, that we may live in the light that shines brightly today, as it shined brightly over Bethlehem, as a Star that night two thousand years ago.

That we still hear the truth in faith of that joy of the night when our *God* turned on that light and know in our hearts the face of our savior and his eternal life light. The one that said to me, *I Am he*, of whom he said, said he. Praise our Lord, our God and the star he gave us on that night he gave the world light two thousand years ago. He really wants you to know he loves you; remember he washed your feet when he was thirty-three years old; if you don't know him, you've never lived.

Ask *Jesus* into your life that he may give you, *life*; he said to tell you that, yes, he's talking to you.

MOTHER
MOTHER'S DAY, EVERY DAY

I thought I'd write a love note to you today, as I have some things I need to say before time passes on, and I don't get to say what I want to say to you today.

I love you dearly is the first thing I want to say, which is something that I've never said enough to you, and I want you to know that I do know that too. Every day should be *Mother's Day* for the rest, and the best of your life, because you did such a good job when we didn't know or understand your part in God's plans.

I realize that most people never bother to get around to ever saying just how much they care, so I'd like to take the time for all, to say how much we care and thank mothers everywhere for all they share and give to this world we know as life. Again, thanks, Mom.

I place my God in high esteem at this time in my life, and I'm sure I will for the rest of my days, I want you to know, I thank my Lord and my God for you in my life, as well as how proud I am that you call me son. I may appear to be a failure to some and of no account to others, but in my Lord's eyes I'm doing just fine; so have faith you will always be able to be proud of me.

I may never be rich in this world I'm passing through, but I did become wealthy with God and life; that's treasure in heaven to me. So I want you to know as I watch this pen in my hand that my Lord, Jesus, is alive and well with us, for God gave his son that you may have one that got covered with some of his heavenly grace. He wants you to know that I did remember to say, I truly love you and he loves you too.

To *my mother*

P. S. Grace to your family tree!

SELF-PORTRAIT

Do you see difficulties in all that you do, or is the door of opportunities always open to your line of sight?

Life is all about what we see and hear and of our efforts to be what we would like to see us to be.

So here's a truth for you, my friend, if you want to wake up and join the ranks of the living once again! Joy, it's the "oh boy" of the day in everything you do or say.

Alter your life by changing your attitude! Those who do well as opportunity offers are sowing seed all the time to help someone in some way and will never have a need.

You see, people are lonely and hurt because they build walls instead of bridges. Remember what happens around us is outside our control, but the way we respond is in our control. All people respond to a smile in any language.

One of the best defenses is joy. Be happy, be simple, be cheerful; of all the things you wear, a smile is most important.

Be somebody to be proud of; remember, a light in the manger shined back at the star in the sky. For spilled on this earth are all the gifts of heaven. The list is quite long—joy, peace, happiness, and also opportunity. All we have to do is open our eyes and see!

One thing I need to make clear, attitude is like altitude; you need your head up in the sky so your ears can hear and your eyes can see. Just what it is you're trying to be. Because if you don't listen and what it is to be, then the Lord will say, "My friend has no need of me."

True today, my friend is he who receives a benefit with gratitude, repays the first installment on his debt. Every man works in his life is a picture of himself.

Praise the Lord that he likes what he sees. For to be honest, you need the opinion of a friend. Ask Jesus if he likes the picture that he sees you to be and forgives where you've been.

Amen
A Friend

SEEKING

Ask, it will be given, seek and you will find, knock and it will be opened. Is this a house, or is spoken of about life? Think of these are these footsteps. That our God has given to you and me? Do we open the door of life and see all the gifts that he gives? That we may go in and have abundance of all that. He wants to give. Or do we stand in fear, afraid to enter a door that our God and Lord has placed in our sight for us to see, to have, to enter, to be.

God wants all of his children to live in abundance and to give to others as they see a need. For if you give as you see the needs, then he will give you more, so you will see more need. Give freely as I give to you. If you do this for one of mine, you will never find lack in this love of mine.

Seek first the kingdom of your Lord, your God. Ask of his spirit. Seek his truth, and this will bring honor and glory to your soul, for all to see. Yes, seek the kingdom of his love, and you will see his love from above. You will see the dove of your God's love descend and pour from his cup. The sight of the kingdom and the gifts of his love!

Seek and receive. Ask and believe. Knock, the door of the Lord is for the lost and forlorn and all that want to come home. Come to the Lord, I've heard it said, but it sticks in my mind that statement that I hear him say, "Seek first the kingdom; you will always find me at home."

I heard him say today, "Seek me with all your heart, you will find me and you will never again be alone. For your clay vessel I use as my throne."

For if you seek me, you find the kingdom. If you seek the kingdom, you also find me. Seek, I heard him say.

BELIEVE

See to believe, the blind could not see, yet in our Lord Jesus they believed that he had the power of God to make them see. Even before he gave them the sight to see!

The deaf hear God when he speaks in their ear. How is it that they can't hear what we want them to hear?

Why, is it those of us that say we can see, can't really see some of the things we would like to see? Do you think in our Lord's wisdom, he whispers in our ears? You're not really ready to get a glimpse of me. So not today can you yet see of me. Or is it the fact that spirit as he is, we are not able to see him as a living tree. We're not used to talking to a tree, but how about your neighbor, the same guy you and I can see. In him can you see a look that looks like Jesus, my Lord, looking back at you and I? Maybe we can see Jesus in some of us, if we'd take the time to really see.

I don't mean to say it's hard to see all the nasty weeds growing around those good-looking trees.

Mostly, what I'm trying to say is that, he's telling me is that maybe, sometimes we just have to believe what we can't always see. The same goes with hearing or I should say not hearing (*deaf*) they can still believe. The blind they can still have strong faith, and still not see the main teaching. Here is to learn and discern as hope, faith, and love. The greatest of these is love, also known as truth, and in truth of God. Your Lord loves to give to those who believe.

Truth, honor, glory, and life eternal in these! You can't see them, but in these you can believe. For God's words are these: Ask to believe, believe in life believe in Me, I heard my Lord say to me.

Believe, I Am he

THE
VICTORY
VICTORY

I let it be said once. I may appear to be a failure to some and of no account to others. But in my Lord's eyes I'm doing just fine. So have faith, you will always be able to be proud of me. My answer to the question is in Jesus Christ our Lord (1 Tim. 4:16). Christ guarantees our ultimate victory.

Only by choice can each and everyone miss the victory party with the Lord. To a new young Christian, let me state it in terms you will understand. Our greatest victory to me is the salvation of eternal life won by Christ and given to us, you and me.

God equips us with all the armor and weapons we need to defeat the enemy and his temptation (Eph. 6:10-18, 1 John 5:4).

We must realize to experience victory in the Christian life. We must be willing to commit ourselves to faith of our Lord and not backslide in to sin again. The Lord has already said he conquered our enemies and, in fact, the whole world (John 16:33).

But I must say to be true and fair in God's own way, this is what he said to make quite clear, "If we confess our sins to him (in prayer), he is faithful, true, and just. He will forgive us and cleanse us from all wrong" (1 John 1:5-22).

I prefer a lighter note when I try to relate what he has said or what he wants you and I to say or do, but learned that I do best when I tell it his way and write what he wants me to make this pen say. So he says it this way, "I will never fail you. I will never forsake you" (Heb. 13:5).

The real fact of life is, I gave my only son to die in this world that you might live, then I raised him to life that again you might live (John 3:16)

I say again, there is only one way to God's great house. My son is the path, also the guide of your way to come to me, *I Am* is the truth, the light, and the way.

I say again, *ask. I Am* will show you the way, *today.*

"*Victory, I Am*"

In the light of truth, *I Am* the morning star. In the light of the silver moon, *I Am.* In the light of the dawn of the sun, *I Am. I Am* the Lord of all creation, *I am* he.

> *I Am Victory*
> *Holy, Holy, Holy*
> *I Am, Won*

A STEP

Again I am sent to spread my ink, to tell the world of the word, to seek the lost that they be found.

Those who become Christians become new persons, implanted of the Holy Spirit. They are not the same: the past is lost, the future found, the old life is gone; a new life has begun. Speak truth and honesty, are you in a new life with Christ? Hold the truth dear to your heart and guard it with your life.

Because of the promise of God made of the covenant with his son, being crucified on the cross and giving up his spirit, for the love of mankind we put our trust in the Lord and God from above. That we might share in the promise of love that he has poured on us all from above. By his grace you stand to share his love. As a new life given from above, ponder on this amazing grace he has poured out on you, that you may stand in the very sight of the Lord your saving God.

For he chose us, from the beginning, and all things happen just as he decided very long ago. (Eph. 1:11).

Don't take lightly the new life God has given to you, for you will face his fury if to him you don't stay true. For as I said, "Guard his spirit with your very life and his word speak out that it may be heard to help another be found today."

Once you were doomed forever because of your many sins, as the world following the prince of the world (Satan), ones that from God had turned away. We were born with an evil nature under God's shame, saved only by asking for his eternal life and all of his gifts.

Sing out his joy, put praises in the air, for now that you've found him. He'll never let you down. Remember to pray each and every day. See, you become a part, a step in the path that he calls his way.

I Am the *truth*, the *light*, and the *way*. That's what the Lord Christ Jesus came to earth to say. Love your neighbor as you love yourself, for *I Am* with you in all you do and say.

That's what I heard him say today!

FATHER

My God, how deep is my humanity? How deep the recesses? How large the pit? How wide the crevice between sin and God? I have the need to know of this thought called life that you have given to me.

How small we are, how large all that we can see, and larger yet is the vision of things yet to be!

My God it scares me, the thought of all that you've given to me. It scares me to even think of all this love you give to a lowly person like me, and yet I know you can also quickly take it again from me. I fear the Lord, my God, even in my own backyard and will give you praise all the rest of my days. For when I was young I knew no fear, only worldly things did I hold so dear, I thought that I alone sat on my throne. I thought that I had done it alone and then I fell to the bottom of the pit, lost and alone, not even solid ground. I heard you say, "It's okay *my son*, take my hand, this is not the end, for I'll be with you clear to the end. Then eternity, my *son!*"

Be silent, know *I Am* God. Stand and be known *I Am* here. Learn of me and follow my ways. Take my hand as we walk this land. Hear and see. I'll tell you what to say, to the people along the way. A student learns from his teacher. A Father's joy is his children that they know the Father and know they are one, not to be lost along the way.

Joy is my name, and today I have come. *I Am* the path of light; truth and honor are my delights. Come with me, I will show you the path, and lead you along the way. This I heard him say to me this very day, today . . . !

I refresh the humble and those with repentant hearts, new courage. Today is my Father's day. The Father and I are one (Isa. 57:15)

The Holy Spirit spoke, I respond.

FATHER'S WAY

In the way of my Father *I Am* in him, in him I will be all that *I Am*.

In the will of My Father *I am* in his way, in his will *I Am*. As my Father goes, I go that way, if my Father says stay, I stay. If my Father says go that way, I go. I know not his mind or his way, I find it strange to say *I Am* the way, for I only go my Father's way.

You will hear people say we know his Father yet not know his way. Many will argue or confuse, distract, or lead astray, only I know my Father, only I know of his way. For if you know my Father, you know me, and if you know me you have seen my Father. My Father and I walk this land. My Father and I from the sky descend and ascend only in the word of my Father. Do I have the right to say, "In my Father, *I Am* only then from his word? Do I have the privilege to say *I Am* the way this day?" For his Father said, "This is my beloved son, in whom I Am well pleased" (2 Pet. 1:17). Walk my path the steps are smooth, and I'll show you the way today. I also say *I Am* the truth and the life and the light that shows the way to my Father.

Follow me today I say *I am*!

NOTHING FOUND

Let's talk about nothing. I had it all, good times were always to be found. Married with a beautiful wife! Dancing on top of the town! The good things of life, amazing when you think of them now!

The children of course there with the wife! You look around and think of the clown that let you down, your best friend till he made off with your wife. Next thing you know they come and stole your car while you were sitting in the bar. The banks are that way when you forget to pay. And when they call, you can't be found. Now it's the house, that dirty louse, that's all he could say, "If you don't pay I take away because you're six months late as of this date." Now I sell the house.

Now it's today and time to pay for all the fun you've had in your life. No money left to be found, so you can't be seen up town. The bill collectors know you can't even play around.

All out of money and no honey! With no money, no place to lay my head down! Guess then, no hope left, the ears have all turned deaf. It's been short and sweet on the way down to defeat. What a story I could tell. Too much dope, too many pills, can't carry on and pack this heavy load. I have fallen to the bottom of the pit. No one to hear when I holler with fear down here in this place we call hell.

So I call Jesus, do you know this forlorn and lonely man's name? I search you out, I seek your face in my time of trial and need, "Would you bother with a man such as me?"

"I hear you when you seek my face. I see you when you enter my space" (Jer. 29:13). "When you ask, I hear!"

For I know the plans I have made for you. They're plans for good not for disaster. To give you a future and hope when you call on my name, when you turn to me in prayer I will listen, I will always be here.

I will end your captivity and restore your place and honor. You'll find me when you seek me and look for my face.

The Holy Spirit speaks of I Am, the man, Jesus, my Lord, says, "He is that man, I Am. Come follow me, I will lead your way, this day.

"Nothing lost, nothing found. Eat my bread, drink my wine. Today, you have been heard and found . . . *grace*."

SWEET DREAMS

What's in a dream? Is it a look into the future or a look back in the past, or a way for God to say you're alive today? What's in your dream? Is it what it seems or is it a bad scene in the middle of a scream? A dream is not always what they seem, but often they're all they seem, and much more. So open your mind and look at the score, what's the vision of all the unseen things we try and see in one night's dream?

What's the picture of a lifetime of dreams unseen? You're a record of thought from the one that creates such things. For when you create all things you also direct the creation of your love. That's the thought of love sent from above in a message of thought of what or not is in keeping with his way, within the boundaries of his love. For remember, he is a God of love and good tidings. His wrath remains outside of his love, which brings the nightmares or thinking outside of the scope of his love. The evil of the heart of man is trying to work the plan of darkness. The deep recesses of sin pledged to every single son of man, which gives man the choice of living with God or by the works of man in the dark of night.

Makes you wonder about the very thought of living a dream and why some are good and some are not. What you call a dream, God explains the making of and thought of a dream. In fact, if you ask in earnest, he will dissect your dream and explain all that's in the dream he made out of love. If it's a dream of love sent from him above, it's a light of love. For if it's not of him, you really don't want to let it in, for its not the way of life, for death may appear in darkness, to the reader I fear, if you don't take the time to say "none of you" with will I do, if not of love and my God.

So just let me say, a dream is a scene of the movie of life you go to.

If you don't like the dream, take a look at what it means. With God it's always a dream if you know what I mean, for he only shows the path of life and says, "Follow me. *I Am* the path, the way, the truth, and the life."

Turn on the light, "sweet dreams."

VICTORY WARRIOR

My God, what more can I give to man? What more can I give for another? I raise my hand that I fight for this man. I raise my hand that I may fight for this land. Some people believe it's their religious right not to fight. Yet I know my God says, "I have the right to fight for what is right." My Lord gave me a sword that I may strike the darkness out of the night so that his people may see his light and take hope and have faith and join the army of God and do the right, to act, to charge, to win. This is not a race to win, this is a fight to win, that the power of God above and his undying love, with the death of his son, gave us the win over death and all the sickness of self within.

We have the God-given right that we can claim the highest mountain and claim the heavens for our Lord in his name and might. That all the world and heavens may see that this earth he gave to you and me! We have the sight to see into the future and to claim all his love. He has said, "No greater gift can man give for his fellow man then his life." But it seems to me, you can also give your enemy your love sent from God above, to overcome your enemy with God's love and make that enemy a friend. For in things I've learned on this world I'm passing through, is that once you make a friend, you no longer have an enemy trying to harm you and may even try the good life, stuff that holds with God's thought of all men are created equal. That all mankind have the right to life in the name of his son! So my thought stays with my love of God, give me liberty or give me death and victory to the son, the Lord Jesus Christ, the holy righteousness of God, the *I Am* of all that says death is where your victory, I give life eternally and abundantly.

My warriors live forever and never strike my sword at the least discord.

God leads the charge, his son, *I Am*, is the way, the life and the truth, the great glory of God.

I Am victory, said *I Am*.

INDEPENDENCE DAY

What in the heck you suppose could happen on a lazy day like the Fourth of July, when everyone's eye is looking for the fireworks in the sky? Mind you not the kind you earn but the kind you buy, to make the Fourth of July some kind of treat. Independence Day is not the kind you buy, the one they fought for back then, when they lived and died for the day you call the Fourth of July. The guns went boom, boom, boom, the rockets burst in the midnight air, the flash of war across the sky, the men to arms to do or die, that's the one remembrance brings to me.

The ships on fire at sea, the cannon balls taking the rigging down, never a doubt they got in but they won't get back out. The British have fought and lost the fight in time to come. They will wish they had won. Just the same, it will make the world a better place for the new country to breathe and live in one they can see to dream in, of a dare to think of home and land. A republic if one can stand. A country free to do God's will. A land to light the light on the mountain hill, to tell the oppressed of the world!

Freedom rings, we have beaten the king; we fought the fight and won the dream, that's the Fourth of July and what it means. From sea to sea and all the in-between, that's what this day means. All for one and one for all! The trinity of our Lord, God, and Holy Spirit, live in this land, that to me makes Independence Day.

If you haven't had the chance to see it yet, maybe you should try opening your eyes and see what you can see.

Lord Christ Jesus said, "This way, today, I have come to save my people, those whom can hear, open your ear, the time is near. Those who dishonor the Lord should have great fear."

The kingdom of heaven is at hand. I have this land in the palm of my mighty right hand; again I say fear, if you hear the Lord, your God.

I Am said.
Friend

Sea the Sun

Have you ever thought of heavenly things, the thought of God and angel beings? Have you ever bothered to ask if you might see or to touch and feel the things you can't see? Like grace given to the undeserving, like you and me, the day that Jesus died. Yes, you and I were given grace and still receive his grace to this very day. For until we come and ask to be forgiven, we can never stand without the blanket of his grace, we can only stand and knock on his door with faith in our heart and humbly ask in faith for his grace and the right to stand in the presents of God.

Think on this, in this world of the see and be God's grace. Is it something you can see? Your faith I should see, that's what he's telling me, for by faith we should ask of Christ, through his spirit the grace of God. It's like seeing the air you breathe or the sun rays that darken your skin, to know in your heart that you are one with God. Two thousand years ago when Christ Jesus was crucified on the cross, he said, "Forgive them Father they know not what they do." Not knowing they were really crucifying the son of God.

Two thousand years have come and gone. They buried him in a borrowed tomb. Of course, the sky went dark that dreadful day. Satan thought he had his way. The stone rolled away the morning of the third day, and lo and behold, the birds sang and Jesus up and walked away, then he told his friends, "I truly am, the truth, the light, and the way."

They saw him and believed. What do you see? What do you believe? I ask you truly, "Do you believe in me?" That's what he said to me. So I ask you today, what is it you see? To believe the son, the morning star, the rainbow, the thought of love blown on the wind! Here today then gone away only to come again and bring a new dawn.

I come to say to you this day, feel the touch, use your mind to see, use your faith as a mustard seed. Ask the mountain to throw itself into the sea. Know *I Am* with you, then. You will get a glimpse of Me. Ask, believe in me.

Two thousand years, you still can't see, but if you try, will you feel me. I'll show you the way, if you ask of me, today.

This I heard him say to me today. He said to say to you today. "Come follow me." He said, "*I Am a friend.*"

Thank You Note

I have a need today, to talk to the son. My spirit wants to talk, just to tell someone. Yet I'm not in a hurry, for I learn of his ways as I pass through my days, that to hurry him is just a whim and does, nothing to mend your ways.

I'm talking to him as I use my pen, for the ink he gives me writes quite clear. I'm use to writing to people here or over there, for he asks me to write to them so he doesn't have to shout what he has to say, for he has to talk in lots of different ways. Because he has a message and has quite a lot to say, but thinking of the short span of time he also uses this pen and ink of mine, but I'm not talking to people today. See today is Sunday and I need the time to pray, that's what I meant to say.

I'm used to writing to people telling them what he has to say, that sometimes I just want to say sweet nothings in the ear of my Lord and to thank him for the promises he just seems to make appear and the little gifts that he leaves for me every now and then. All the times I'm in a situation and need some help or maybe just a friend.

To tell the truth, I believe this is the first time I've ever tried writing to him.

Just seems to me that's what you do for a friend, write a note and let him know you just happen to be thinking of him. Grace is the place to wait for him. I thought I'd just share this little note to all of you out across this grand land, that our Lord's alive and well and thinking of each of you. If you want a hand shake today, well, "brother," just hold out your hand.

Thank you, Lord Jesus, this is what I wanted to say, thank you comes from lots of us, for making life so grand in this great land.

America, together we stand in our God-given grace land.

Lord, hope you read this note I wrote . . . !

WAIT

Wait, wait, wait on the Lord to cross the fiord, wait on the Lord to bridge the cleavage of hell, sin, and God. Wait on the Lord I say, for your daily ration of bread. Wait on the Lord to show you the way, so you don't get lost and not be found. Wait I say on the Lord.

Wait, that seems to be the word of the day, so I Am says. Wait, the secret to this, is this, he's never early. He is never too late. He is always right on time. If you will learn to wait, another word for that is patience.

A mortal man is in a hurry to his life, it's a race, death catches him, and he forfeits his life.

Hence, wait on the Lord, he calls out to his lost sheep or rings the bell, only the ones close to him can hear or see. The rest have to wait until he comes close to them before they can hear him and see. Nice trick, for a Lord that only lets people see him as its time and as he wishes for their lives, because in truth we are dead until the Lord your God and Father say you are alive. Wait, I can hear him say, "Now if you are reading this, you understand the word wait." So will he change the word for you? The new word is watch, in other words, pay attention to the happenings of the Lord, in that I mean, he's always with you if you will watch, "pay attention," listen for his sign and manner, "watch" the way he moves around through you and others. Watch and listen to the Lord; he's alive and well and will show himself to you if you will only ask. Watch, and listen. Love from above will land on you like a soft, light rain. You will know it's for you as an expression of his love to let you know he is the way, the truth and the life. The real life that comes from him!

The real love, the real peace, the only grace!

Then he said to say "tell them I am he of whom he said I Am. My name is love."

A Friend

The Last Man Stands

I have come to declare this day, a warrior I Am, wounded of man. I still fight for my clan.

I am a soldier of the good old USA. I fight for the right that says all good men are free. I fight for the right of freedom as well as our liberty. I am wounded and dying that my loved ones may have the choice, the chance to be all that. God said they may be. That founded this nation and set us free. The God that said you can "trust in me." The one that said believe, with my mighty right arm, I will overcome.

Yes, a warrior I am, as long as I stand, I will fight to the death for all I believe and when the fight is over. On death I will still stand, then raise my sword and stand as a man and declare for my God that gave his son, to die for the likes of you and I. To my nation that believes all men are created equal that believe truth, honor, and integrity come to the love of man. Down to his own clan, his family name to hold in high honor, to know the high truths of God, as he bestows on us his great plan.

Eternal light, salvation, life eternal to the very last man!

I am from a strong and far-off land. I am the bright morning star. My home is far away across the golden sand. Yes, I Am an ambassador from sea to shining sea and all that will ever be.

I hold these truths to be. My peace I give to you, not as the world gives, my peace. May my joy fill your heart! I call you friend and give you a promise, I will always be there for you, I will never leave you or forsake you.

I am he of whom he said I Am. I am with you always, even to the end of the age (Matt. 28:20).

Anything is possible, if one believes (Mark 9:23).

Yes, I Am a soldier, a warrior to say the least, I fight for God's love sent from above. I fight for my king, that I may give you his love.

A Friend

GOD'S LOVE

The deep of depth may not be sounded or measured. As the depth of, God cannot be found. Searched for but not found. As the love of God cannot be comprehended! Nor can you watch the son and walk in darkness. For once he has chosen you and turned on your light, you are his and you walk in his light and shine out to others that they may find their way to the Lord to find their own light that he freely gives just for asking.

Amen

A GREAT BEACON

The word is a great beacon that shines across this great land.
The word is a light that searches the hearts of man.
The land is the Lord's. So pick up your swords, come follow the
    Lord.
For we hear the cry to battle that I so plainly see.
To arms, to arms, I can hear the cry.

RAY OF LIGHT

Tonight is the fight, a heartwarming battle. It's all about the darkness and mad as Cain can be. The devil is complaining that the night is much too bright, since the Lord Jesus turned up his light. For the day is to come, so say some. The darkness will fail and flow into the lake of hell. That will be a warm night for some. If they don't climb out and grab a ray of light and not be quite so dumb. But I can't see. That's not for me. I come for my Lord that I might save me some amazing grace. Some are too dumb to run. Just hold out your hand. You say come. Finally, some of them see it's white as a light if they get close. Then they see what with all that light and all that's bright. The darkness flowed on into the sea. So no more darkness, night, and fright! Somehow, it got flooded with the Lord]s blinding light. So say good night with your light. Give this other guy a flash of light or maybe a key and a kite. The Lord's got lightning and thunder. He'll get the fight tonight.

JESUS SAVE ME

I asked Jesus to save me
As he lay dying on the cross
Lord of lords.
King of kings
The messiah of many,
And all things
This day,
I give you my very best.
That on your day
You may give me
Your rest
Thank you, Lord Jesus
Amen

A Call to Arms

Let me tell you, my friend, a story of where I've been as I watch up here in the sky.

A call to arms a call to arms, I hear him telling me. Love is from above. The rest is lust of man, you see. In the summer night, I see the flash of light and know he is speaking to me and the rolling thunder over yonder I hear him say, "'tis of me."

Truth, hope, faith, and trust, he keeps telling me. For from above, I've been washed with his love and much more. Now I can see the words that he gives to me. I heard somewhere my father places words in the air that I may see them there. They are words to share.

He heals with love. Look for the dove or a feather floating through the air. "Believe" is his cry for the likes of you and me. For its life to believe and death for the grieved and those that just wander on by.

An Oath

This night I will take an oath, a pledge, even a decree, of truth faith, hope, and of course, most of all, my love.

Please hand me my sword as I place my hand in a glove. For tonight, this night I ride on to battle, I'm riding for my Lord. My king is ready and waiting and helps me to fight the good fight. I don't dare dishonor my Lord. For in the midst of battle, I will cry out loudly, "I come to fight for my king." There I will defend his honor from all those below. It's time to mount the wind, the clouds are rolling in. I may well die in this battle. This fight I find us in. But there will be hell to pay, I swear, this day. Damned if I'm giving in.

My king's the thing, and his kingdom is within each and every heart and stout heart.

He died for us all, rather than let us fall. So I place my trust in him. The least I can say is if I should die this day, it will have been for him.

It's a secret you know. I heard it straight from him. He's alive and well. He and his Father are staying at the inn. So I'm here to say I may fight another day, because when I saw my Lord, Jesus, as he was heading on his way, he said, "We'll not fight this today; it's more important you pray. I've already defeated them." Amen.

A MOTHER'S SON

A mother's son, I feel I can speak, because I am one.

Through the good times and also the bad! A mother is always the best friend a son ever had. In times of trouble, she always there, when you've been bad! You can feel that stare in the back of your head. Remember, but I can think of a few. Then the proud times when you get married or when you have a kid, you'd think it was her day to sit on the throne.

Yes, not much, a mother won't do! When it comes to her son! One she loves never forget without a doubt, she would lay down her life and ever die for a son or two. That's a mother, and I'm sure you gave one too. Times to remember that, old friend call your mother, tell her you love her. Then call her again.

A mother has eyes in the back of her head and no matter what was said, she knows just what you said.

As I was musing, taking a walk the other day, I thought of my mother.

HIS SON

Walk a mile then smile. Tell a lie. Sit down and cry. Contrast of life. A picture of God at work with his potter's clay! Another still shot of a child at play with a ball of clay. Both with the thought of love from above! When he gave his son some clay and sent him to earth, because his son had a message of life. He wanted to say to the people of that day which resounds to this very day (believe).

That's what Jesus preached. He wanted to show people of his Father's great plan to gather all people to himself in a way that we could see God walking among the people as the son of God. To be received to the Father, following the path and teaching of his son. Jesus said, "My Father you can't see. I say believe, I am the truth, the life, and the way. None can come to the Father except by way of me."

The truth is no one can enter the kingdom of God without being born of water and the spirit. The Holy Spirit gives new life from heaven as the wind comes and goes. So is the working of the Holy Spirit the way of his son (John 3:5). As the Father goes, so goes the way of the son. Salvation comes on the trail of the bright morning star.

The same Jesus that makes the claim, my Father and I are one.

This is what the Holy Spirit had to say this day, "believe" we are one.

HELP ME, LORD

Help me Lord, help me through this test. Tell me my work, Lord, and I'll do my very best.

Be, loving Lord lead me to do your best. Yes, tell me, Lord, that I may tell the rest that we may praise the Father and with the son have a day of rest.

Yes, tell me, Lord, what you would have me do for you. Rekindle your fire, Lord. Shine your flame anew. For the word I say this day. This day I save for you. Hold me, Lord, as this day we start anew.

Amen

Finger of God

Today is a new day. One of the last, so the word of God says! The last days will come like a whirlwind, blowing here, and back again. People doing the things they always do. Climbing the world's mountain's trying to get to the top. Just to see it's really not there. The answer to their dreams! Gone like vanishing cream.

The devil is out there telling all that will listen. "I will give it all to you if you will only kneel and worship me." The great deceiver still busy living a lie, still promoting his own counterfeit dream. For if you will eat of his apple, he will think I have them in my grasp. They won't even see me as a snake in the grass.

Yet in the last days, the Lord Jesus is standing his army, pointing out his finger on the hand of God, saying to his people those he calls his own. His chosen people if you will. He points his finger at the likes of you and me. Then says in your heart, "Come and follow me, leave all behind that you thought you ever knew. Leave it in the dirt where you stand. For the clouds of God are forming, thunder and lightning will fill the air! The Lord will roll his thunder. The finger of God will fill the air.

The thunder of God will say, "Satan where are you? Who is it that I should fear?" I created heaven and hell. I decided long ago when I pointed to hell and the lake of fire and told you then you would rule only down there. I alone claim my own. My choosing if you will, that will fear only the Lord their God and have life eternal, filled with love" (Ps. 22:27-28).

So stand in fear if you see the finger of God pointed at you. Ask forgiveness and kneel to him. Praise God as you worship him. Then praise the son, again and again (Mark 10:17).

Remember sinners, Jesus already knew the power of his love went out to you when he said, "I love you child." Then pointed his finger at you!

This is as I've been told this day, to pass on to you with this pen in my hand, as I help the Lord as I hold his hand to point his finger across this great promised land.

Remember his cross then make you stand. (Rom. 6:23).

Christian I Am

COME TO LOVE

Come to love. Come to grace. Come to God. Take your place

His kingdom has many mansions waiting for those that have eaten of this truth. The blood of Jesus flows all about the place never to be enmity of his truth and his grace. His love is eternal with flow of amazing grace. The ship is soon leaving, hurry aboard and take your place. Jesus is captain of the helm. The treasures in heaven, silver, gold and jewels, and the goodness of God in abundance lying on the ground! To be rich in heaven, you only have to look around his house on the mountain, his diamonds in the sky.

This truth for you is clear for those of you that hear. Hark, aboard the ark, lift up a mighty cheer. Listen for the whistle, but most of all in your joy and cheer, humble yourself a little and remember the name and the grace that got you here. In your thanksgiving and thank the Lord, your God, you didn't have to drink of his cup of fear as he brought you to this place of grace and drank the cup and sail it is finished.

Love, grace, and my Father are finally here.

Lord Jesus, help me in this I plea, to know your way as I walk through my day.

Help me, Lord that I hear your word and give me light that I may do what is right. Help me, Jesus, in all I do. Talk and walk with me as I walk your way. Take my hand as on the mountain top we survey the land and you, the promise.

If I Didn't Care

If I didn't care,
Could I really feel this way?
If I didn't care,
What would I do with my love?

Would I keep the my promise
That I made from above?
Would I have even gave
The light of the day,
To show you the way!
God, the Father
Has guided from above!

I'M WITH YOU

It's time to get going. I'll be at your side. Pick up your head, smile inside.
Know I'm with you in that have some pride.
Glory, with the Lord, son, at the start of each new day! It's a great place to stop and pray. So stop and smell the flowers and linger along the way.
Talk to people about me. I'll tell you what to say.
You're whole life before you at the start of each new day. Just ask the Lord to help you and guide you all the way!
Thank you, Lord Jesus, I truly pray.
                              Amen

GOD SPOKE TO ME

I am he of whom
He said I Am.
            Amen

Hearsay

Kindness is a language
Which the deaf can hear
And the blind can see.
They both see and hear
The Lord Jesus
When he gets on his knees!
Pray the Father to hear
And to see!
Praise the Lord
And know that it be.

THE WAY IT IS

The way it is, a reality check is what he has given to me. That I write

With, my pen to pass on to you. For as he asks of me! He will also ask of you.

The Lord speaks of time bygone, and what he says is like song. To remember once back when! Before you lived! Before you remember! Then his son, he gave for you, as the people of the world, hung him on the cross. They said, "Away with you."

That was way back then. But he forgave us of our sins and the name of today is the here and now, look around.

He went away, but not for long. He came again to that third day and talked to his chosen that he told to come along so they could witness. He's been here all along. He rose to the Father that third day and spent some time praying as he went on his way. You see this was all part of his Father's plan to give a new covenant. That his son could walk the land and have fellowship with mere mortal man! For God made us mortal man out of clay. To have the choice to fall and die or walk the land that he made when time began. Yes, I'm here to say, "Sin is still with us and will still try to stand as a mortal man."

Jesus, our Lord, said, "I hold the keys of hell and give life eternal to those whom drink the water of my well. A mortal will die and fall in the sand, to love only once and never rise again."

The choice is yours. Choose as you please. Then remember he holds the keys. Yes, look around.

The time of the end draws ever near, he asks again, "What do you want? The choice is yours."

He made it very, very clear, "Come follow me."

He is the beginning, the here and now as well. He is also the end. He is the ring of life if you follow him as he promised. Your life will begin again.

That's, what I heard him say to me this day. That's what I give to you. I have nothing more to say, accept, "have a nice day."

A Friend, a provider of the way!

A Thought of Eternity

The Lord blesses me as I write this thought to you. For I write what I hear him say as I write this thought. He says to give to you about taking the time to write to you. Love is all we have. That's the total gift of God, the Father, his, son for his people. That they may be found worthy to be in the very presents of God! For all eternity, he wants to love us and doesn't like to live alone.

Remember, his voice speaks from the faces of a thousand men, so that his word maybe heard. His word was voices of a man two thousand years ago. Jesus said, "I Am the word of God."

His voice is still heard to this very day. Listen, I can hear him say today, "Child, I still offer eternity to you to this very day."

I cried out. None was there to hear. I looked about. Yet none was there to see. I wonder, have all in my distress gone and deserted me? I moved about, felt a thorn in my side, I realized a man had done this to me, for an arrow was protruding from me. Is this my brother that has fallen next to me?

I cried in terror, now afraid that someone might see my fallen brother. A comrade and me, I said "Lord, I would forever have your love if you would give me this thought that you call eternity."

SEE

Don't lose vision I give so free and clear. Hold on to faith and truth that I hold so very dear.

Time will tell if what I say is true. For all, this world my peace I give to you.

A promise is made I give to you: here in this life, I will always be true; here in this life, I will always do for you (Matt. 7:7).

My peace that I give, wear like a ring and know in your heart it's a song you may sing.

Remember child, in this life you're passing through, I'll never forsake you, and always be there for you. That's God's promise that he just gives you.

Time will tell just who goes to hell, not one of mine that hear the shepherd bell. They know my voice and can safely tell the bell I ring is the same as the song I sing! Come follow me to the house of the king.

The vision I have that I hold so very dear. Is a thought of family, the ones I hold so dear!

This is a time of love, snowflakes I can hear. The birds of spring are also very near, I can also see a summer soon to be and stories told to children, sitting on my knee.

Yes, people all I hold so true. There is nothing in this world I wouldn't do for you. So follow me, what I say is true, my Father is the king. His house I will show to you.

Hold the vision. Believe in me. A promise of God. He said to me.

THE SPIRIT HAD HER SAY

This is alive, this is real. To make a choice and know how you feel! The truth of love shines in the night for all sinners that have lost their way and have no defense against the darkness that sneaks around in the middle of the night. The spirits are there for you to discern. For let it be said, "A spirit of the darkness has no light. Yet a spirit of God walks it, the light that all may see the cross on its back that's carried for Christ to those that would choose life." Light and life are as truth today. Ask a spirit of light, hear what he will say. For once you see the tree that shines out in the night. Then you will know the fruit of the tree. All have a word of light or truth of God that comes with his might, for none can stand the come from the darkness of night, unless they have turned on their light.

The lost are found once they accept and turn on the life, the truth and the light of the way. The answer to the question is yes. The Holy Spirit is sent to tell Jesus is alive, Jesus is well. Remember, Jesus and God, are one and the same. The Holy Spirit in a flash of light is all in one the same. God by another name good, truth, holy, what is in a name! The Spirit, of God is always the same. Never doubt the way of the word. Listen to the light. Believe every word, for some of this world this light will not even be seen. Ponder this and see just what does the spirit mean.

Do we live in a dream of do we have a God that can't be seen with eye of the likes of you and me.

The spirit says, "See what I mean. The light of life is of God and only through his some can he be seen. Listen, hear the word he puts in your ear."

TAKE MY HAND

Live at the speed of light. Spread the word. Run to catch Christ of the resurrection, with great joy. Celebrate the dawn of a new day. Pray each and every day. There is not a day he will not guide you along your way if you will listen. Wait and learn to discern the coming of the new dawn, the beginning of a new day, a walk of life, it can't be told in a better way, in a better light that the light that Christ Jesus can bring into our lives, each and every day.

Remember that the truth of Christ, the very truth of God's love begins each and every day with the Lord. The living prop of his walk on this earth as a man, stands on the seashore each day in your mind and learn of his ways. Climb the hilltop at the start of each new day inside your private room. Open your heart to God. Ask the Lord to lead the way with each new day as you stop to pray.

The light of dawn will strike with a bright light of you to your heart. Pick up his sword. Do your part to spread his word, try to do as you know he did. Perfectly!

For me, this day is his message of truth that he has said to say. Listen to his word. Learn the words of his way. Rejoice that you have found the path of his way. That you may learn to discern, for wisdom comes to those that hold on to his hand then stop and think. His hands are serving hands. His hands are helping hands. By the power of God above, we have his love, his gift. Son of love to love!

Spread his word, shed his light, for he makes each new day out of the darkness of his night. Then remember, he said, "I Am the way, and my peace I give through grace, yet we live."

I heard him say this thought for today. Love yourself this day as well as your neighbor, shake his heart as you shake his hand. My Father and I are one. Take my hand, sins I erase, and give life in their place.

A Friend, I Am

THANKS IN GIVING

Father, I ask that I may give you my weakness, that you may give me your strength. I ask that I may give you my doubts that you may give me your belief. I ask that I may receive and that you may give me the forethought to discern and seek. I give you praise that you make me weak that I may see your strength in my eye.

I ask for life that I may see my Lord's face, that I may hear and see the light and the path. The where and the why!

I ask all these things that you may share all you hold dear and of worth with me in your life. That you gave to me through your son that I may see you in all that will ever be through the eyes of your son, a friend that lives with me. I cannot say I speak for me. The face of your son in spirit speaks for me in faith of the path that I am honored to walk with him and bask in the sun of his very bright light.

I do not claim a life with him. I claim a life for him that he may walk his life in me. That he may talk to his own. That he knows by name the ones that are lost and forlorn. The poor and the maimed, the sick, and the lame, all that are sinners that he has come to claim. All that can hear his voice. All that have, tears in their eyes. The ones that turned away and forgot how to pray! The where and the whys!

For I can hear him say this time again forgive their sin. That they may see my light and put faith in truth and not in might! Praise them Father for I died for them. Now I claim them as mine that I may live in them.

Thank you, Father, we win again and today I walk with men.

I heard him say, to him.

I AM, SAID HE

Read this now, this is true.
I am the spirit of Christmas, the Christ-must tell of the things he heard in heaven. To convey to those he loves.

Read this, this speaks of love. The spirit of God, with my hand spreads this ink all across the land, that some will know, that some will see this hand writes what the spirit wants to tell. For those he wants to hear and see.

Didn't you ever read in the Scripture? The stone rejected by builders has now become the cornerstone. This is the Lord's doing, it is a marvelous thing to see for the likes of you and me.

What do you believe the owner of the vineyard and press will do? Looking down from the lookout tower and see into every county, into every little town. Trick question, who are you trying to fool? Mark 12

Whose picture and title are on the coin? Then give to Caesar what belongs to him, but all that belongs to God must be given to God.

Your problem is not knowing or reading the Scripture. You do not realize the power of God. For when the dead are raised, they will be like the angels in heaven. So then as for the dead and the living, the Scripture states that God is the God of the living. I Am the God of Abraham, the God of Isaac, and the God of Jacob! God is the God of the living in the writings of Moses. God said, "I am there as I am here."

Remember the widow gave her all. The most important thought is the commandments. You must love your God, your Lord, with all of your mind and all your strength. The second is this, love your neighbor as yourself, none is greater than these.

With that the spirit said, "You are not far from the kingdom of God." Beware, because of this the punishment will be the greater for those that don't see what the spirit says, "To hear and see, be true to me!"

THE WALK

When you go there, do people stare at you?
When you speak, do people listen?
Do they walk off and leave you standing there?
Do you like people to intermingle with you?
Do you pretend they are not there?
And look at them with a blank stare?
And wish they would go away?
Or say I just don't care.
I can't help you and go on your way.

What do you think of yourself today?
Did you take the time to pray?
Did you thank your God for your family and friends?
Did you ask your Lord to walk with you today?
To guide you right as you go on your way?

I wonder if you asked him,
Just what he has to say about your walk?
Would he say, "I had a fun kind of day today.
As we went along our way!

I talked to some people and listened,
To what they had to say!
Oh yes, I did help a couple
As we went our way today!
Remember, Jesus said,
"Follow me, I Am the way."

GOD BLESSED AMERICA

God blessed America when he gave it to our forefathers and said, "Make this country free." The people of France gave this country the Statue of Liberty, to be a guiding light for all those who would be free. At what cost are freedom and liberty given to you and me? Many men have fought and died to keep this grand land.

Listen, I will tell the story as it was told to me. Told for those that would reach out and feel and see!

At the top of the stairway stood the Lord and he said, "I Am the Lord, the God of your grandfathers, Abraham, and the God of your father, Isaac, the God of your Jacob as well. The God of the living! The ground you are lying on belongs to you. I will give it to you and your descendants. All the families of the earth will be blessed through you and your descendants. What more, I will be with you. I will someday bring you safely back to this land. I will be with you constantly, until I have finished giving you everything I promised."

INDEX

I was a Viking once, way back
    when, 126

J

Jesus, if you have a need, 44
Joy to the world today, 22
Just the thought of God, scares
    some folks, 75

K

Keep your sights high if you
    expect Jesus to come into
    view, 101
Kindness is a language Which
    the deaf can hear, 163

L

Let me restate what has been
    said for nearly three
    thousand years, 23
Let me speak this day of the land
    of God, 34
Let me tell you, my friend, 153
Let's talk about nothing, 139
Live at the speed of light, 168
Lord, I feel so lost and alone, 85
Lord Jesus, your disciples, you
    sent to all the earth, 84
Love a little, Love a lot, 65
Love your neighbor as yourself,
    goodwill toward men, 39

M

My God, how deep is my
    humanity? 137

My God, what more can I give to
    man? 142
My light flashes across the paper
    and writes a message, 112
My pen ran out of ink, 89
My time with you, most of you
    are short in a span of time,
    73

N

No matter how much we
    struggle, 25

O

Out of the dark of gloom, 92

P

Pray in the will and love of God,
    56

R

Read this know, this is true, 170
Red skies in the morning, 69

S

See the corruption that has
    spread across this land, 119
See to believe, the blind could
    not see, 133
Simple words as I think of you,
    104
Sometimes when you're feeling
    blue, 110

CPSIA information can be obtained at www.ICGtesting.com
Printed in the USA
BVOW011800160912

300401BV00002B/41/P